A Sense of Place

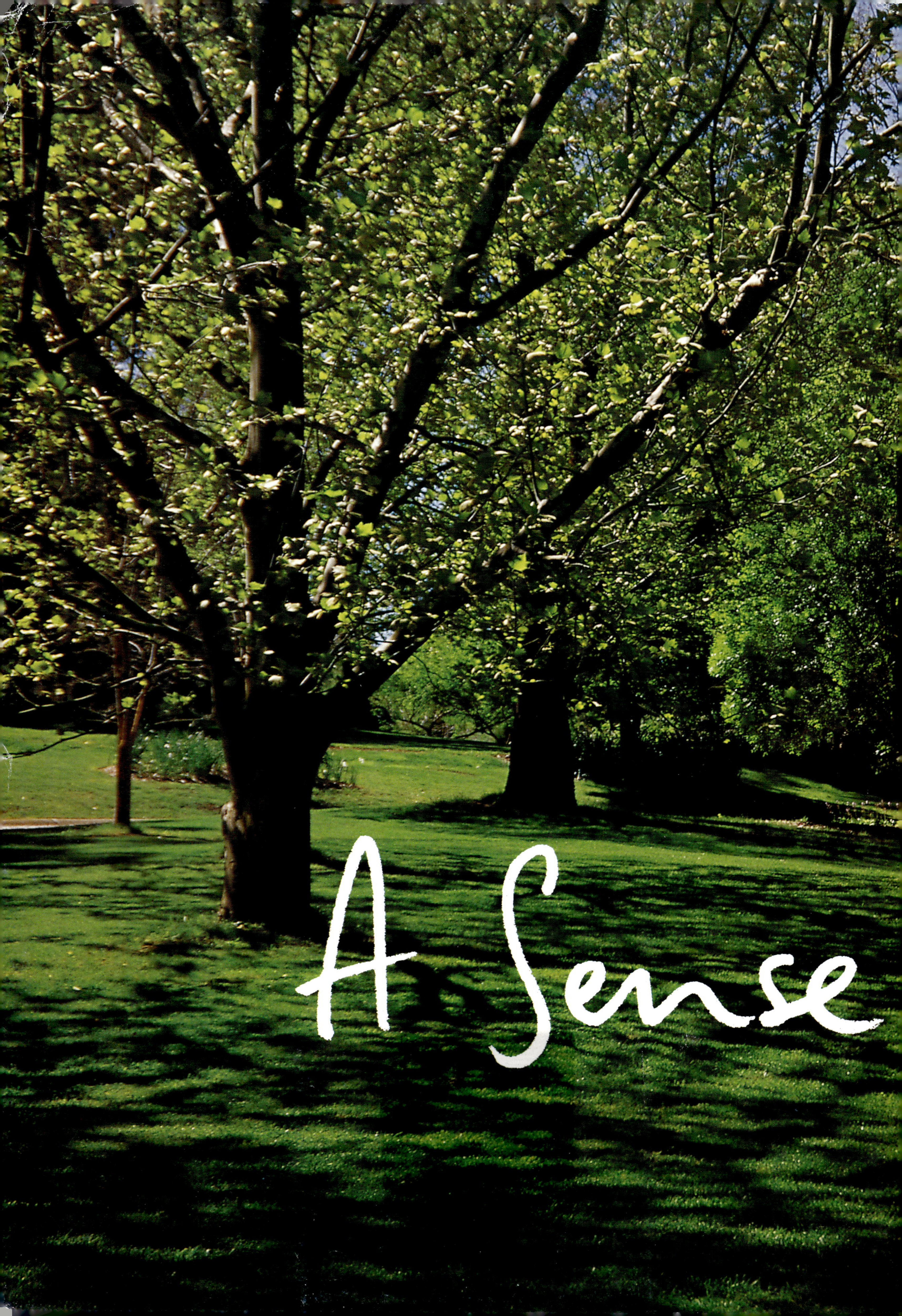
A Sense

THE GARDENS OF
ANDREW PFEIFFER

of Place

LANTERN
an imprint of
PENGUIN BOOKS

PHOTOGRAPHY

Andrew Pfeiffer: pages i–iii, vi–vii, x–1, 7, 8, 13,
15, 18, 19, 20–1, 24–5, 30, 35, 36–7, 40, 41, 44,
74–5, 76, 78, 79, 80, 81, 82–3, 84, 85, 86–7, 88,
90–1, 92–3, 95, 96–7, 98, 99, 100–1, 102, 103,
104–5, 106–7, 109, 110, 112–13, 114, 115, 116,
117, 118–19, 120, 122, 124–5, 126, 128–9, 133,
135, 136, 137, 143, 146–7, 148, 149, 150–1,
152–3, 154, 155, 156–7, 158, 159, 160

The author and publisher are grateful to the following
photographers for permission to reproduce their work.
The author would also like to thank Ms Candy Le Guay
for permission to reproduce three photographs by the
late Laurence Le Guay.

Balthazar Korab: pages iv, v, viii, 46–7, 48, 49, 51,
52–3, 54, 55, 56, 58, 60–1, 62, 63, 64, 65, 66–7,
68, 69, 70–1, 72, 73
Laurence Le Guay: pages 4–5, 10 (author as a boy),
11 (author's parents on knoll)
Scott Cameron: pages 16–17, 22, 38–9, 42–3, 138–9,
140, 141, 142, 144–5, 166
Jerry Harpur: pages 26, 31, 32–3
Joanne Morris: pages 27, 28–9
Craig Kinder, Gale Force Photography: page 77
Ignacio Naon: page 127
Andrés Sánchez: pages 130, 131

LANTERN

Published by the Penguin Group
Penguin Group (Australia)
250 Camberwell Road, Camberwell, Victoria 3124, Australia
(a division of Pearson Australia Group Pty Ltd)
Penguin Group (USA) Inc.
375 Hudson Street, New York, New York 10014, USA
Penguin Group (Canada)
90 Eglinton Avenue East, Suite 700, Toronto, ON M4P 2Y3, Canada
(a division of Pearson Penguin Canada Inc.)
Penguin Books Ltd
80 Strand, London WC2R 0RL, England
Penguin Ireland
25 St Stephen's Green, Dublin 2, Ireland
(a division of Penguin Books Ltd)
Penguin Books India Pvt Ltd
11, Community Centre, Panchsheel Park, New Delhi – 110 017, India
Penguin Group (NZ)
Cnr Airborne and Rosedale Roads, Albany, Auckland, New Zealand
(a division of Pearson New Zealand Ltd)
Penguin Books (South Africa) (Pty) Ltd
24 Sturdee Avenue, Rosebank, Johannesburg 2196, South Africa

Penguin Books Ltd, Registered Offices: 80 Strand, London WC2R 0RL, England

First published by Penguin Books Australia Ltd, 1999
This paperback edition published by Penguin Group (Australia),
a division of Pearson Australia Group Pty Ltd, 2006

10 9 8 7 6 5 4 3 2 1

Cover design by Patrick Leong © Penguin Group (Australia)
Text design by Ellie Exarchos © Penguin Group (Australia)
Front cover photograph by Joanne Morris
Back cover photograph by Balthazar Korab
Typeset in 12.5/18 pt Centaur by Post Pre-press Group, Brisbane, Queensland
Printed and bound by South China Printing Co., China

National Library of Australia
Cataloguing-in-Publication data:

Pfeiffer, Andrew.
 A sense of place : the gardens of Andrew Pfeiffer.

Includes index.
ISBN-13: 978 1 92098 947 7.
ISBN-10: 1 92098 947 1.

1. Gardens – Design. 2. Gardens – Styles. 3. Landscape gardening. I. Title.

712.6

www.penguin.com.au

To Hugo and Jinty

and in memory of Rosie Baldwin

Contents

To build, to plant, whatever you intend,

To rear the Column, or the Arch to bend,

To swell the Terras, or to sink the Grot;

In all, let Nature never be forgot ...

Consult the Genius of the Place in all,

That tells the Waters or to rise, or fall,

Or helps th'ambitious Hill the Heav'ns to scale,

Or scoops in circling Theatres the Vale,

Calls in the Country, catches opening Glades,

Joins willing Woods, and varies Shades from Shades,

Now breaks, or now directs, th'intending Lines;

Paints as you plant, and as you work, Designs.

Begin with Sense, of ev'ry Art the Soul,

Parts answ'ring Parts, shall slide into a Whole,

Spontaneous Beauties all around advance,

Start, ev'n from Difficulty, strike, from Chance;

Nature shall join you; Time shall make it grow,

A Work to wonder at — perhaps a Stowe.

AN EPISTLE TO LORD BURLINGTON [1731]

Alexander Pope

the
GENIUS
of the place

Horace Walpole once said of William Kent that 'he leaped the fence, and saw that all nature was a garden'. Today we need to do the same for entirely different reasons from those of eighteenth-century England. Then, European thought placed mankind at the centre of the universe. Consequently the English landscape garden and its idealised compositions represented a conquering of, rather than a reconciliation with, the wilderness. It is one thing, however, to conquer the wilderness and another to destroy it. Since the beginning of the industrial age human beings have stepped well outside their natural niche to become the most populous animal on earth. Our impact has been such that controlling the world's population and restoring as much of the natural environment as possible will undoubtedly be the greatest challenges of the twenty-first century.

Gardens should once again imitate nature. But instead of creating gardens based on some imagined, Arcadian ideal, we should base our gardens on the original, indigenous environments that once existed where our own gardens now stand. In order to do that we need to have an intimate knowledge of all the natural qualities of the site, from its underlying rock to the quality of its light in different seasons.

I find that I garden best when I take the time to listen to the subtle messages of the *genius of the place*, and when I allow the site and its surroundings to determine the character of the garden. Whether designing gardens that use indigenous or exotic plants or, more commonly, a mixture of both, I first determine the character of the natural habitat — or habitats — that I will be working within. I need, for instance, to be aware of the topography of the site and the way it has influenced the soil and ecosystems that have developed upon it. I can then decide what mixture of plants I shall use. It is better to use exotic plants that are suited to the habitat than to use native plants that are not.

As a landscape designer, my first responsibility is to relate my gardens not just to their *existing* surroundings but often to the *original* indigenous qualities of the site. No matter on which continent I am working, I like to have a reasonable idea of the character of the site and its environs when it was once a wilderness. This is not simply an indulgence. Making the effort to discover what the natural environment of the garden and its surroundings once were enables me to understand the fundamental qualities of the site.

This means that when designing a small garden for a brownstone house in New York, for example, I am interested in the natural history of that small patch of ground and its neighbourhood. I think of the native trees observed by Robert Juet, an officer on the *Half Moon* in 1609, when Henry Hudson made his famous journey up the river that bears his name. Juet reported that there were a 'great store of goodly Oakes, and Wal-nut trees, and Chest-nut trees, ewe trees, and trees of sweet wood in great abundance'. Indeed, much of New York was covered in a spectacular forest — including many immense white and red oaks, tulip trees, liquidambars, dogwoods, wildflowers and grasses — so sweetly scented that Daniel Denton, an early resident, wrote, 'The Countrey itself sends forth such a fragrant smell that it may be perceived at sea before [ships] make the land'.

Such information is the key that unlocks for me the magic of the wilderness that once existed. Whilst we no longer personify forests and streams with particular gods and goddesses, we acknowledge that each place, however large or small, has its own particular individuality making it different from any other place on earth.

Although most of the gardens in this book look as though they each possess an entirely different character — as though each one is derived from a different style — in reality that is not so. Whether the gardens be formal or informal, or whether they find themselves in subtropical or temperate climates, I employ the same basic principles in every case. After learning about the endemic qualities of the site, I next choose the plants I wish to use according to stringent rules of ecological compatibility. The result, when I'm successful, is the sense that my gardens have sprung spontaneously from the earth. To further enhance the feeling of harmony I choose plants — whether they be trees for a forest or perennials for a border — on the basis of compatibility of leaf colour and contrast of texture and form. Ideally my intention is to achieve a simple but rich tapestry of foliage. Less important – because it is so ephemeral – is flower colour. But it too must be related to the natural light and the surroundings so that, for example, the colour of the flowers won't clash inadvertently with the colour of a nearby wall. Thus, in the end what might appear to be an extremely simple, perhaps ad hoc, composition is actually highly disciplined. Perhaps the greatest lesson I have learnt over the years from studying the work of Capability Brown is to hide, as far as possible, the evidence of my own hand in the landscapes I design.

Most garden designers work within limited geographical areas of much the same climate, and this gives their work an immediately recognisable consistency. Through various accidents of fate I find myself working all over the world, and in doing so my gardens are composed of a widely divergent palette of plants and building materials. Apart from the local climate and quality of the light, I must also be aware of such things as local building traditions and the scale of both the garden and the wider landscape beyond.

As far as I am concerned, the question of formality and informality in a garden's design is a secondary one. Level and terraced sites, or those with consistent planes, can suggest formal treatments, just as an irregularly undulating site almost certainly demands to be treated informally. The style of the house or building around which the garden is being designed will also have a bearing on the matter. A symmetrically designed house might suggest exciting possibilities for a formal garden. Although the expression the *genius of the place* has traditionally been used solely in connection with the landscape garden, I think it can also be consulted to determine whether a garden should be designed formally or informally.

The mere idea of formality is shocking to many natural habitat gardeners because it suggests the intervention of man and his sense of order. But we must never lose sight of the fact that gardens are there to give pleasure. They should never lose a sense of theatre, and they can even evince a sense of humour. If they fail to give pleasure then, I suspect, they ultimately fail to qualify as gardens. Contemporary natural habitat garden design in the United States and Germany sometimes results in gardens of the most admirable intentions which nevertheless inspire little more than tedium.

Creating idealised, informal landscapes based on natural habitats, within which there will be formal elements, perhaps best describes my style of gardening. It is, after all, a natural human instinct to revere the wilderness whilst at the same time wishing to impose order upon it. I do not think we shall ever separate the one instinct from the other – although we must control the latter. My gardens are thus an interpretation of the way I see mankind's ideal interaction with nature.

Gardens have always represented more than simply the way we plant the ground. They reveal the state of our relationship with the natural world. It is for this reason that we need to know what distinguishing features once made, or make, our original natural environment so individual. And we should always be aware of the possibility of introducing some of those very special, localised qualities into our gardens.

And if we look – and learn from what we see – it is possible to do so.

PREVIOUS PAGES *It is better to use exotic plants that are suited to the habitat than to use native plants that are not. Around a polo field in New South Wales, formal lines of exotic trees were planted, which are compatible with the surrounding endemic trees. The exotic trees echo the rectilinear nature of the field, leading the eye towards the impressive hill beyond.*

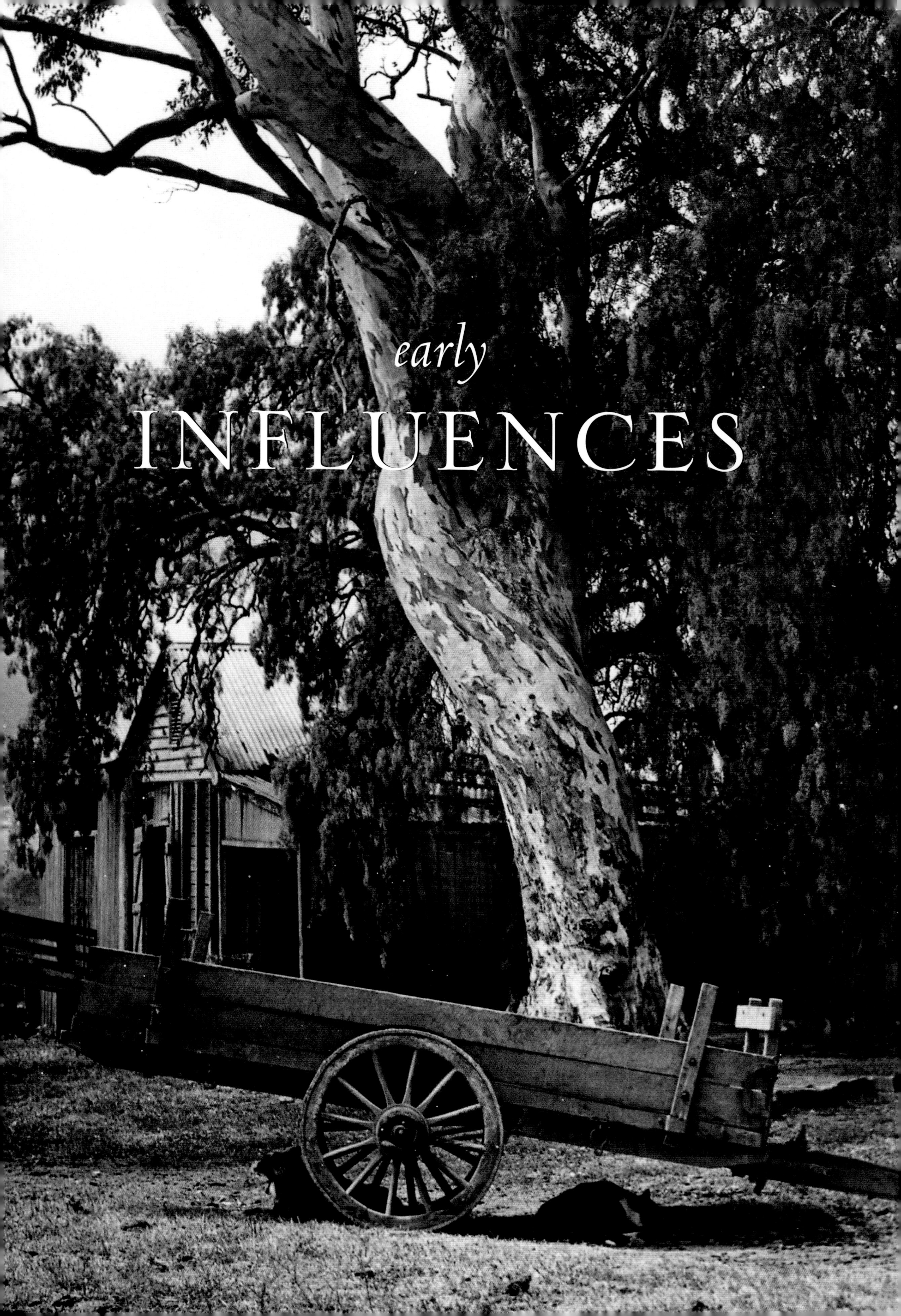
early
INFLUENCES

When I was very young, my family would spend weekends during the warmer months of the year at our house at Palm Beach, some fifty kilometres from Sydney. This was long before Palm Beach became a Sydney suburb. Pacific Road was a sandy lane over which *Angophora costata* trees created a canopy. These trees also grew in our garden of largely untouched, native bushland.

The angophora is a gum tree, similar in appearance to a eucalypt. Its pink trunk and limbs will often twist into unexpected shapes which — to the fascination of my two brothers and myself — parody naked human forms in the throes of ecstasy and agony. As if to substantiate the latter impression, angophoras drop sap of the deepest red which will stain concrete garden paths and quickly claim them as part of the bush.

Our house was on the summit of the Barrenjoey Peninsula and looked east onto the Pacific Ocean and west onto the magnificent landlocked section of sea called Pittwater, beyond which lay the dense, untouched bushland of the Ku-ring-gai Chase National Park. Smaller trees, *Banksia serrata* — their large, leathery, indented leaves and grey woody fruit also fearsomely animate — grew amongst the gently overlapping shelves of pale sandstone. On some of the larger and flatter rocks in the garden were ancient Aboriginal carvings, the only permanent marks left on the landscape by a people who had lived there in harmony for some 20 000 years.

Various kinds of eucalypts also grew in the garden, and in them we often saw koalas. Large black currawongs would dive amongst the tree tops, their haunting call charting the cubic acres of air above. And raucous kookaburras alighted on our breakfast table on the terrace where we fed them pieces of chopped meat.

In the morning light of summer at Palm Beach, there was an incredible vibrancy of sea and sky seen through the branches of gum trees. By midday the bush would pulse deliriously with high-tension waves of energy emitted by cicadas in the trees. These were days when the threat of bushfires was great, the tangy scent of the bush hanging heavily in the air. And at night, as you fell asleep, you heard the muted roar of the surf on the beach below.

These few distant memories have helped make indelible my love of the Barrenjoey Peninsula. In those days, with a child's natural optimism, I took it for granted that the rest of the world had the same unspoilt beauty and sense of limitless pristine space.

My awakening sense of place was given great impetus while I was still very young, when we went to live in the Bega Valley, between the Snowy Mountains and the ocean, 500 kilometres south of Sydney. In Australia what is called an estate in England or a ranch in the United States is called a *property*, unless it is in the Outback where it becomes a *station*. Our property, which is now my brother's, is in a corner of the immense natural amphitheatre which constitutes the valley, only a few kilometres from the mountains and dominated by a high pyramidal hill, or knoll, the remains of an extinct volcano. From its summit the entire Bega Valley can be seen. On clear days, over a range of wooded hills to the east, the Pacific Ocean appears as a long, thin and distant band.

The property was called Greenmount, supposedly because of the colour of the knoll. But during that first summer nothing was green as we found ourselves in the middle of a drought. The main house on the property was a large, rambling bungalow built in 1928, and far better suited to a suburb like Sans Souci or Moonee Ponds than to the Australian bush. Its garden was far too small and characteristically surrounded by a prim, neatly clipped privet hedge. This further enhanced the impression that it had been plucked by giant hands from the concrete of Australian suburbia and placed as a practical joke in the most unlikely of rural settings. It was, after all, a twentieth-century addition to a landscape that had been laid out in a remarkably sympathetic fashion in the nineteenth century. In fact everything else hung together so well that the entire property was — as a result of a felicitous mixture of design and accident — virtually a landscape garden. Roberto Burle Marx, the Brazilian landscape designer, said that a garden is 'a construction, like a novel by Dostoevski or Tolstoy. They knew how to capture a climate, to dramatise certain moments, to emphasise. It's the same thing in a garden: how you conduct the spectator to see the same thing from different angles'.

At Greenmount from the moment you enter the front gate and cross the wooden bridge over the river you encounter striking elements of an ideal Australian landscape garden. As the drive wends its way towards the house, up and over the hills and along the ridges, delightful pictures compose and recompose. One moment the eye is carried to the horizon and the next it is preoccupied with incidents along the route, such as a copse of native trees or an ancient eucalypt overhanging the drive with a superbly arching bough. Much of this is accidental. But great thought obviously went into the placing of buildings and exotic trees. English oaks thrive in the Bega Valley and at Greenmount they beckon you to visit their shade, each rewarding you with its own distinct sense of place. The branches of ancient deodars sweep to the ground over a roughly hewn post-and-rail fence, their sap and resinous cones filling the air with sweet scent on hot summer days.

It has always struck me that the balance between exotic and native trees is well tuned at Greenmount. In general, the native trees overwhelmingly outnumber the introduced species. It is only in close proximity to the houses and farm buildings that the exotic trees exert a strong influence.

As might be expected, the majority of native trees at Greenmount are gum trees. So unique is the character of gum trees that it is the contrast between them on the one hand, and exotics and other native trees on the other, which gives the composition at Greenmount both interest and tension. Just as Capability Brown juxtaposed native oak trees and exotic cedars of Lebanon for much the same reason, so at Greenmount might exotic oaks have been planted in close proximity to native *Eucalyptus tereticornis*. Perhaps the greatest value of such contrasts is that they paradoxically enable us to see each individual native tree more clearly, thereby enhancing their significance in the composition.

The large, evergreen rusty figs, *Ficus rubiginosa*, also grow at Greenmount on the steep sides of the knoll. These natives, with their rounded crowns, are not unlike English oaks in silhouette. The underside of their crowns is evenly cropped by the cattle, and this line mimics the steep terrain on which they stand, making them look, from the distance, like

PREVIOUS PAGES *Laurence Le Guay took this photograph of my father, brother Kerry and me at Greenmount, Candelo, in about 1957. An ancient forest red gum,* Eucalyptus tereticornis, *with an interestingly twisted trunk, frames the Myrtle Mountain in the background. Overhanging the wooden shed is a peppercorn tree — a native of South America.* TOP *The native figs that thrive on the knoll at Greenmount are important visually since they act as dark full stops in a landscape dominated by the lighter, airier foliage of eucalypts.* MIDDLE Angophora costata *is a gum tree that often resembles a human figure in the throes of agony or ecstasy.* BOTTOM *An ancient* Angophora floribunda *stands in the foreground of this pastoral scene at Greenmount, whilst in the background are several indigenous forest red gums and a group of deodars.*

slightly topsy-turvy mushrooms of the blackest green. These fig trees create an extraordinary atmosphere. I can well understand why Buddhists confer divine status on their close relation, *Ficus religiosa*, the Indian peepul tree. Even on the hottest day its shade is deep and cool.

Partly because of the figs' close presence, the base of the knoll has always been a place of special character. Here, in a glade between groves of *Angophora floribunda* and partially protected by the enveloping arms of the base of the hill, a cool spring bubbles out of the ground into a deep reflecting pool, before trickling away down a shallow valley. I remember the first day I ever went there, a few weeks after our arrival at Greenmount. It was a hot summer's afternoon and our mother read *Hiawatha* to my brother and me in the shade of a tree. Today when I visit the base of the knoll it strikes me that not only does it have an air of ineffable spirituality, but that its energy had subtly taken possession of me – even as a child – for life.

Into this seemingly ideal life, reality and its painful lessons intruded from time to time. Droughts, bushfires and floods are part of a natural cycle in Australia. During dry conditions apocalyptic bushfires could roar out of the mountains with frightening speed. Clouds of smoke overhead would blot out the midday sun and make the day like evening. I remember being spellbound by scenes of unaccustomed and bizarre beauty as burning ash, glowing in the eery dark, fell around us as if a volcano had just exploded. During wet weather the rain could pour ceaselessly for days on end. Our wooden bridge would disappear beneath a silent and sinister torrent of immense momentum, and the river would rise as much as three metres above its normal level. On the surface huge trunks of dead trees, mostly swept out of the mountains, bobbed along in the boiling current as if suddenly animate.

I began to understand that there were certain limits to the customary benevolence of the land. In addition to its powers of enchantment, it was also capable of punishing with a sudden cruelty those who misread or ignored the immutability of natural laws.

As we grew older, the river at Greenmount became our favourite playground. For several kilometres it winds its way through the farm, tumbling between huge granite boulders, and creating a sequence of waterfalls and deep, still ponds. Over a hundred years earlier, settlers had planted weeping willows at the edge of the stream and by the 1950s some of these were enormous. Indigenous species such as the silver-foliaged ti-tree, callistemons with their red bottle-brush flowers, and *Lomandra longifolia* – clumps of grass with sword-like foliage – also grew by the river's edge. Here the native plants and exotic willows combined to create an effect not unlike that of a classical Japanese garden.

At the age of nine and a half this way of life, which I enjoyed so much, ended abruptly when I was sent to boarding school in Sydney. Had I not been sent away, I would no doubt have wanted to remain living in the Bega Valley for the rest of my life.

When I was fourteen we moved from Greenmount to Cloyne, a sheep property on the treeless Monaro plains, more than a hundred kilometres inland from Greenmount. Having climbed the Brown Mountain, and after the village of Nimmitabel, you gradually emerge from heavily timbered country onto the Monaro plains. Few native trees grow here and it has a harsh appearance to the newcomer, rather like the higher parts of Andulusia in Spain. The European settlers brought exotic trees with them and so the homesteads and shearing sheds are lost in forests of pines, elms, cypresses and robinias, which give protection from the westerly winds. The rivers too are threaded with poplars and willows which turn a cadmium yellow in autumn. This country, which is both dry and high, is reputed to produce the best merino wool in the world.

Opposite top *Parts of Greenmount were landscaped in the nineteenth century as an ideal Australian landscape garden.* Opposite bottom *The natural landscape along sections of the river at Greenmount – with its rock formations, promontories and banks of shingle – creates an effect not unlike that of a classical Japanese garden.*

The house at Cloyne is also hidden in its own small forest of European and American trees with occasional views out onto the bare, gently rolling hills. The painter George Lambert once said that the line of these, etched against the sky, reminded him of *les cuisses d'une femme*. During the hot arid summers, the garden at Cloyne is a cool retreat from the plains, and when occasionally covered in snow in winter, it becomes a scene of unaccustomed, fragile beauty. Moving to Cloyne meant I was confronted with a totally new landscape and climate at a crucial age. It was easy not to like the treeless Monaro plains and in truth I was initially intimidated by its openness. But gradually I came to see, understand, and love it for its grandeur of scale and serenity of line.

As at Greenmount ten years earlier, my parents set to work immediately on the garden. Cloyne has the advantage of immense trees, several of which had been planted by the French architect Joubert in the 1830s. There was also a series of dry stone walls made from basalt, which had been collected from the surrounding hills, and my parents added to these. Although I preferred to spend my school holidays skiing, trout fishing and reading, I was soon press-ganged into helping to construct these walls. To my surprise I started to enjoy it and eventually began building my own hundred-metre-long wall. Once we turned sixteen, my brother and I were put to work on tractors in the summer holidays, mowing the lucerne, or alfalfa grass, and then raking and baling it. The benefit was that I was allowed to take a tractor and trailer into the hills in my spare time and collect basalt stones for my own wall.

Mitty Lee-Brown, the painter, had returned to Australia from living in France and Ischia and married Bill Gordon. They lived on a property called Bobingah not far from Cloyne. Mitty created an extraordinary house, filled with wonderful paintings as diverse as a Watteau and William Dobell's *Irish Youth*. Outside, she worked with relentless energy to transform a bare hillside into a garden. Bulldozers were employed to create a series of small lakes seemingly overnight and garden walls evolved from nowhere. You would go there for dinner and Mitty, arching an eyebrow quizzically on being asked what she had been up to, would grandly announce in her deepest husky drawl, 'I've been playing with bulldozers *aaall day*'.

After leaving school, and an unsuccessful stint studying law, I read Russell Page's *The Education of a*

ABOVE LEFT *My mother had never been particularly interested in gardening previously, but she and my father developed a mania for it the moment they went to live in the country.* ABOVE RIGHT *Gardening jobs were a chore to be avoided at all costs. I preferred to dam up the stream with my brothers or go for long walks on the knoll with my dog, Peter.*

Gardener. My mother had lent me her copy, which had lain by her bed – regularly consulted – for the eight years since its publication. 'That's it,' I announced on reading it from cover to cover. 'I'm going to England to learn to become a landscape designer.'

My parents were initially sceptical about the wisdom of this move, but I wrote to Mitty Lee-Brown, who was then in India. Her advice was unhesitant. 'Become a gardener,' she counselled. 'Security is for others.'

I arrived in London during a dull, misty week in February 1972, and initially stayed with distant cousins in Cadogan Square. The gardens in the middle of the square seemed so dank and dormant that I wondered whether anything would be capable of prompting them back to life.

Two days later I went to meet Russell Page in his house in Springfield Road in St John's Wood. A tall and impressive figure, I did not find him 'as terrifying as God' as one of his clients once described him. He told me that I could not be a garden designer if my heart was not really in it, and that the only way to test my resolve properly was to work as a labourer in the landscape construction department of a nursery. Once we knew how committed I was to my future, we could discuss the possibility of my going to the Royal Botanic Gardens at Kew, close to central London, as a student. He invited me to return for lunch a week or so later.

He cooked a mixed grill which we ate overlooking his garden. The garden – simplicity itself – was divided into large squares in which he grew a ragbag of plants collected haphazardly from all over the world. I formed the impression that Russell Page was a man of extremes: although gregarious, he was actually quite lonely; although at times impossibly grand, he was in essence disarmingly modest; and while capable of wounding one's pride with a cutting remark, he was extraordinarily generous of spirit. I quickly discovered that few other young gardeners in London could fathom the contradictions of his nature. He clearly terrorised them, and only those who tumbled to the fact that it was all a kind of game remained in touch with him. It was his fingers – long, tapered, capable and sensitive – that more than anything seemed to express his true nature.

With Russell Page's help, I found a job as a labourer in the landscape department at Clifton Nurseries. It was now late March and winter had given way to early spring. All the gardens, including those in Cadogan

BELOW LEFT This photograph of my parents, taken by Laurence Le Guay, captures the rhythm of surrounding undulating hills when seen from the knoll at Greenmount. BELOW RIGHT An aerial photograph of the garden at Cloyne taken shortly after our arrival in 1963. The garden is a forest of European and North American trees, some of which are said to have been planted as windbreaks in the 1830s.

Square which had seemed so lifeless in February, were now coming to life with fresh green leaves and exotic flowers. I shall never forget that breathtaking first spring, and the succession of bulbs from crocuses to hyacinths to daffodils. It was interesting to reflect that the plants which made that spring so memorable – the bulbs, plane trees, chestnuts and magnolias – are all exotics from abroad. None is native to Britain. Yet the authority with which they compose the landscape that is London today is undeniable. Here are plants perfectly suited to the changed, man-made environment that is contemporary London, perhaps the best example being the London plane tree, *Platanus* × *acerifolia*, which is a hybrid of two exotic species.

It occurred to me that somewhere between the stark and uncompromising dichotomy of native and exotic plants there is a midway point where certain plants have to be accepted as *adopted natives*. The logic of this became increasingly inescapable. After all, that quintessentially English story, *The Wind in the Willows*, was named after a tree that is a native of China.

Clifton Nurseries did a great deal of bedding out of bulbs and annuals in window boxes and terra cotta pots for clients in Mayfair, St John's Wood and Hampstead. As the spring progressed, I did more of this and was taught how to position plants in the container so as to create an animated effect. It was an important lesson, since the same basic principle could apply to the planting of trees in a garden.

Russell Page had asked me to keep in touch and let him know how I was getting along. It became almost a routine that I would go for lunch about once a month and he would cook a mixed grill. He had discovered that I could speak some French and we sometimes spoke in that language. It was his way of encouraging me to improve my French, which he considered 'an important part of one's equipment'.

A friend in London, Richard Glynne-Percy, invited me several times during my first year in England to stay on his family's sporting estate at Tomatin in Inverness-shire in Scotland. Here the landscape bore more than a superficial resemblance to the high and treeless Monaro country in Australia. And unlike the over-crowded Home Counties in England, the Highlands of Scotland had that sense of infinite, pristine space which I had come to expect of the world as a child. These were the days just before the North Sea oil boom, and when the Black Isle, which we regularly visited to explore the haunted ruins of Red Castle and the remains of its park, felt like one of the remotest parts of the world. Sometimes we would venture in the opposite direction and swim in the mysterious waters of Loch an Eillan overshadowed by forests of Scots pines and birch trees. And we visited Cawdor Castle, made famous by Shakespeare's *Macbeth*, where, within the walled garden and under the bright July afternoon sun, the herbaceous borders were of a perfection that seemed otherwordly.

The most noticeable thing about the Scottish Highlands is that its people, for the most part, have an incontestably strong sense of ease and belonging to the landscape. In Australia, life is often underlaid by a subconscious confrontation between the European population and their adopted landscape, which is generally comprehended imperfectly. In the Highlands, the Scots pine and silver birch are as ubiquitous as the eucalyptus and acacia in Australia. But whereas the gum tree and wattle are liable to be banned from the Australian garden, in Scotland the pine and birch sweep from the horizon up to and around the house, binding the garden inextricably to its surroundings. Only the most excessive planting of exotic rhododendrons, primulas and meconopsis will rob the Highland garden of its sense of belonging to the natural landscape.

In late October 1972 I went to New York to work for Kerry Fitzgerald and his landscape construction

and maintenance company, The City Gardener. Most of Kerry's work involved making gardens on apartment terraces, high above Manhattan's streets. It was a complete inversion of everything I had ever experienced or considered in the past. These were gardens constructed in the sky and completely disassociated from the ground and natural earth. Apart from the immutable questions of climate, sky and natural light, everything else – including, in many instances, the horizon itself – was man-made. It struck me that this gave the garden designer greater licence to create almost any type of garden which took his or her fancy, since the only remaining quality that might suggest a dubious sense of place was the architectural style of the building. Here fantasy might reign supreme in a virtually unshackled state. Conversely, I began to develop the idea that an almost sacred obligation existed to ensure that any disturbance or cultivation of the natural earth be carried out with the greatest respect. And this strict dichotomy between natural and artificial surroundings – between reality and fantasy – has subsequently become the cornerstone of my philosophy on the making of gardens.

The previous summer Russell Page had introduced me to Robert and Jelena de Belder, founders of the International Dendrology Society, and in early 1973 I went as a student to work in their two private botanic gardens, Kalmthout Arboretum and Hemelrijk, in northern Belgium. Even in those days the de Belders formed the epicentre of European horticulture. I found myself overwhelmed by the botanical knowledge and energy of the de Belders and of my two fellow students: they all spoke a language of plant propagation and Latin plant names which at that stage was beyond my experience. To have been a student at Kalmthout is to have become part of the de Belder family, and their influence on my knowledge of plants and the course of my career continues to this day.

The following year I went as a student to the Royal Botanic Gardens at Kew, which is probably the most important botanical garden in the world. The Herbarium at Kew contains an unparalleled collection of dried specimens of plants – including many of those collected in Botany Bay by Sir Joseph Banks during his voyage on the *Endeavour* – and is one of the ultimate sources in the world of plant nomenclature. Quite apart from this, the botanical gardens at Kew are a magnificent landscape park.

As well as attending lectures every day, I worked for several months in each of Kew's different departments: Arboretum, Alpine, Tropical and Temperate. The Arboretum department covered most of the grounds since it was responsible for the outdoor collection of trees and shrubs. Much of my time in the department was spent cleaning up the Queen's Cottage grounds with two other gardeners, and it was perhaps the most significant of all my student experiences.

It had been decided to rid a large portion of these grounds, which ran alongside the Thames, of all but indigenous plants. Any plant that did not belong to the lower Thames Basin before the Roman Conquest had to be removed. Rhododendrons, chestnuts and weeping willows were felled and burnt, whilst trees such as field maples, ashes and alders remained. Part of a grassy bank not far from the Thames had capsized and the alluvial gravel and flintstones had been exposed. It was fascinating to see this tiny portion of aboriginal London which had remained undisturbed for thousands of years, and to realise the compatibility between the exposed strata of gravel and the plants we were preserving.

After Kew I worked as a student gardener in the gardens of Bowhill, Boughton House and Les Grandes Bruyères in Scotland, England and France. This culminated, in late 1975, in my visit to the French Riviera to work for Charles, Vicomte de Noailles, in his garden, the Villa Noailles. Monsieur de Noailles was in his eighties and a legend in European horticultural circles for his gardens at the Hôtel de Pompadour near Paris, at Hyères and, finally, the Villa Noailles itself.

Perhaps I learnt more about garden design from Monsieur de Noailles than anyone apart from Russell Page. His gardens attested to the pleasure he derived in planning them. They affirmed his belief that gardens should, on the one hand, change the way we see ourselves and the world and, on the other, amuse us. His mind was incapable of harbouring a dry or mundane thought, and everything he designed had a delightfully muted sense of theatre and mystery.

The garden at the Villa Noailles was built on the side of a hill, on a series of olive terraces, where once only a few goats had grazed. There was, however, a spring that produced a hundred cubic metres of water a day, and Monsieur de Noailles designed the garden as a celebration of water in a dry climate. Falling through a series of fountains and ponds, water became the soul of the garden. Murmuring like a furtive conversation in a shady corner or splashing in the exhilarating sunlight, it made certain you were always aware of its proximity.

Monsieur de Noailles told me that whenever he designed new additions to his garden he looked through illustrated gardening books to find the spark of inspiration that would be his point of departure. 'You will find that as your plan develops, and as you adapt your ideas to the site, you deviate greatly from the initial, borrowed idea,' he said.

Accordingly, when he asked me if I would design a pool on the second-lowest terrace of the garden, we first pored over the books in his library together. We decided that, questions of enclosure and scale apart, Lawrence Johnston's tank pool at Hidcote achieved the effect we were after. The surface of Johnston's pool was raised above ground level to create an exciting proximity to the water for those standing at its edge. This was the basis upon which we would proceed. Our pool would be smaller, but anyone walking up these steps towards this part of the garden from the lowest terrace would have the pleasant and surprising sensation of seeing the surface of the water suddenly appear at eye level and, most importantly, within hand's reach. I drew up plans for the pool and did a planting scheme to tie in with an existing olive tree, *Buddleia auriculata*, and a twenty-five-year-old *Beschorneria yuccoides*. Monsieur de Noailles approved of both and called in the builders to start construction. As far as I know, it was the only time he had invited anyone to design part of his garden for him – an extraordinary privilege. On my last day at the Villa Noailles, a morning of brilliant winter sunshine, I went into the study to say goodbye before catching the train to Paris. Sadly, I never saw Monsieur de Noailles again. My next visit to the Villa Noailles was in the spring of 1982, and he had died the previous year.

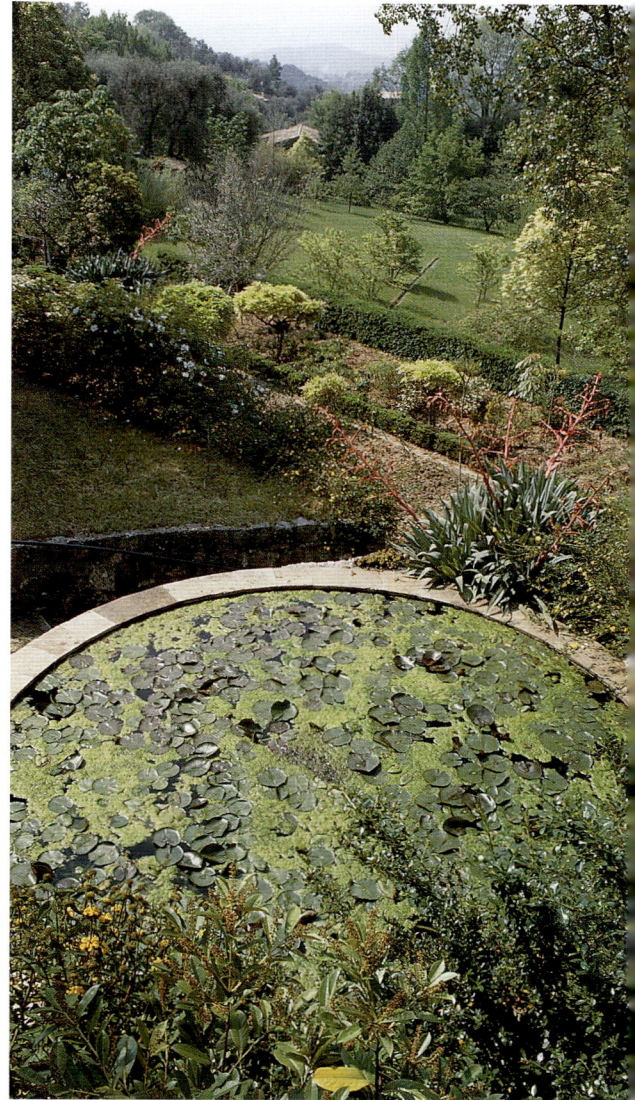

ABOVE *The brief for this pond at the Villa Noailles in France was to create something that would 'give a sense of the exciting proximity of water'.*

a
HARBOUR
garden

M y earliest childhood memories, before our move to the Bega Valley, are of Sydney Harbour. In those days there were fewer apartment buildings and large gardens ran down to the harbour's edge. The house in which we lived at the end of Darling Point had such a garden, and I remember standing on the terrace in the dazzling sunlight of a summer's morning, with the harbour like an immense stage on which the activity of ships and yachts presented a constant spectacle.

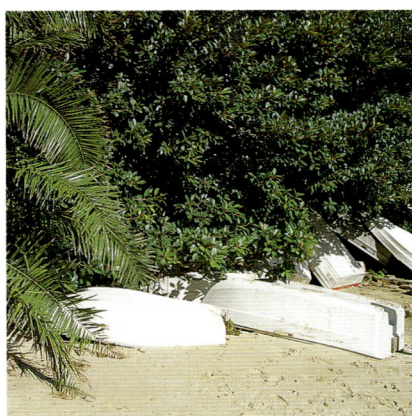

The long water perspectives reaching far down to both east and west, the mysterious slap and gurgle of waves against the sea wall, the welcome shade of a Port Jackson fig, and occasionally the terrifying percussion of thunderstorms which transformed the harbour into a choleric greeny-grey, all helped to instil a strongly defined sense of place.

Ironically perhaps, my first commission to make a garden on Sydney Harbour came to me in England by default. In 1976 Michael Ball, a client, invited me to Somerset to advise on the design of his garden around the Manor House at West Coker, in which Violet Trefusis had once lived. This job was destined never to be since Michael moved to Sydney shortly afterwards. On arriving, he bought a vacant piece of land in Vaucluse, which had previously been part of the garden of a neighbouring house.

Two years later Michael came and saw me in London. He had commissioned a local landscape designer who had unexpectedly left Sydney. Would I consider adopting the Vaucluse project? Michael showed me photographs of his new house, which had been designed by Neil Clerehan of Melbourne. It was a glass-walled pavilion with exceptional views over the harbour, and in particular Watson's Bay. On arriving in Sydney some six weeks later, I saw that the garden sloped down towards the harbour, from which it was separated by a six-metre-high sandstone ledge. This created a dramatic effect and I felt lucky to be given such a spectacular place in which to create my first garden in Sydney.

Originally, the site of the garden, just above the sea, would have been open forest with tall trees of *Angophora costata*, red bloodwood, *Eucalyptus gummifera*, and black she-oak. But these had all long since been replaced, mainly with exotic trees. The original soil composition had also been lost as a result. Although at depth the ground was still sandy and well drained, on the surface it was richer in humus and nutrients than the endemic plants ideally would have enjoyed.

I initially considered replanting endemic trees on the site but a number of factors mitigated against this. In front of the new house stood a group of mature cocos palms, which Michael did not want removed, particularly as the trees had played a crucial role in the siting of the house. These palm trees were not compatible with the idea of an indigenous garden.

Moreover, the notion of a native garden was an unattractive one to my client. He felt the majority of Australian native gardens were untidy and unresolved, and in my opinion he was right. This is because most gardens made up of Australian native plants are designed without regard to these plants' original habitats. Just as a rose and a rhododendron are ecologically incompatible and should not be planted together, so too should a *Banksia serrata*, which likes sandy, acid soil, not sit next to a *Eucalyptus gomphocephala*, which is a native of the coastal limestone soils of Western Australia. Being ecologically incompatible these plants will create a subtle, but nonetheless destructive, sense of disharmony if planted together. On the other hand, the indigenous plants in the sculpture garden at the National Gallery of Australia in Canberra have an unquestioned sense of belonging together simply because they are ecologically compatible.

In Michael's garden, the only endemic tree of any character was a large Port Jackson fig. This grew at the bottom of the cliff on the edge of the harbour, and could be visited by way of steps and a path carved into the sandstone. Unfortunately, the top of the fig had been pruned level with the top of the cliff so as not to interrupt the view from the house onto the harbour. Although barely noticeable from the house, it was an enchanting tree.

In their native state on the harbour, Port Jackson figs are often found growing in rocks a few metres above the high-tide mark, where ground water seeps from fissures in the sandstone. This habitat is naturally quite different from the open forest and light sandy soil that once existed at the top of the cliff. By happy coincidence, however, Port Jackson figs need much the same amount of moisture as cocos palms. Thus the man-made and artificially watered habitat that enabled the palms to thrive in front of this house was similar to the original native habitat on the water's edge.

Taking my cue from the compatibility of this existing relationship of trees, I proposed to Michael that I envisaged the garden as a seemingly chaotic subtropical rainforest, not unlike a painting by the French Impressionist Henri Rousseau. I particularly liked the idea that these rainforest plants would frame the glass walls of the house and lead the eye towards the harbour.

To this end, we further enriched the soil with manure and humus, while over the following weeks I spent much time in Sydney's Royal Botanic Gardens finding inspiration in the exciting subtropical plants which clearly thrived there. Unfortunately very few of them could be found in commercial nurseries. Undeterred, we scoured the specialist nurseries for suitable plants and ended up with several large specimens. Amongst those were *Dracaena marginata*, pandanus palms, some rare philodendrons, *Phoenix roebelenii*, *Strelitzia nicolai*, *Brugmansia suaveolens*, bamboo and several different types of Hawaiian hibiscus.

In their natural habitats, most of these plants are found along the drier verges of rainforests or on the edge of the sea. It made them ideally suited to the garden. Since it faced the harbour, and was only about fifty metres deep, the garden more closely resembled the wind-tossed edge of

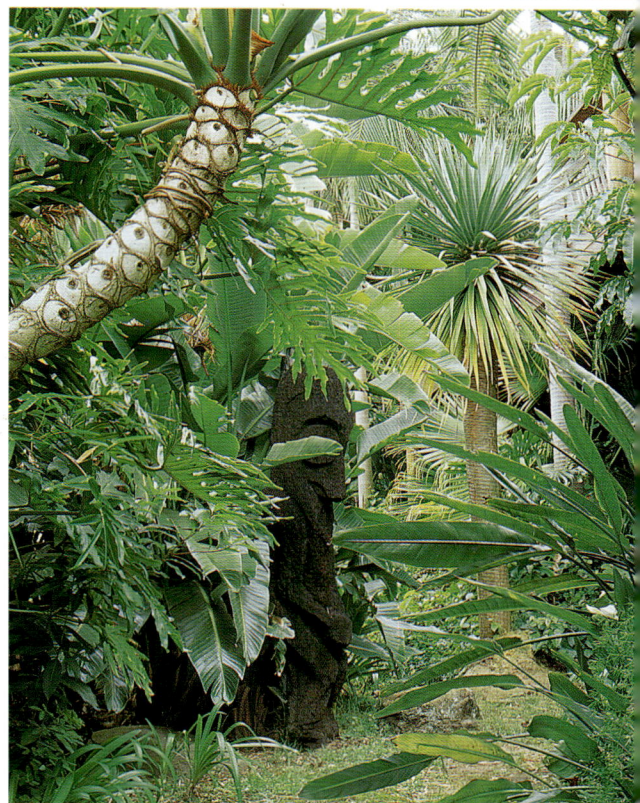

PREVIOUS PAGES *It was important to keep the colour of the foliage of these exotic plants as restrained as possible so as to ease the passage of the eye from the garden, through the opening, and onto the harbour.* TOP *A muted sense of excitement is created here with the greatest simplicity as two young* Dracaena draco *trees grow up between the foliage of a* Strelitzia nicolai. ABOVE *Adding greater excitement, and an air of mystery, is a sculpture carved from the trunk of a tree fern from the South Pacific islands.*

[*19*]

a rainforest, rather than its heart. Obviously those plants that faced the sea had to be tolerant of tougher conditions than those further back in the garden.

We positioned the plants with this in mind. But it was also important that our planting create a subdued sense of excitement in different parts of the garden. This excitement had to be very carefully balanced so as not to upstage the harbour view. The principal means of achieving the balance was to ensure that all the eye-catching plants we used had green foliage. In this particular garden, the mere hint of differently coloured foliage or variegation would unnecessarily catch the eye and hinder its smooth passage towards the harbour.

Furthermore, it was important that all the flowering plants we chose had flowers that were close enough

ABOVE *Seen from the harbour, the garden keeps the secret of its subtropical rainforest garden reasonably well. The large endemic Port Jackson fig, around which the dinghies rest, takes precedence in the landscape.*

to each other on the colour spectrum to be harmonious. This would also help maintain a subdued air, as opposed to using contrasting flower colours which would create a more startling effect and distract the eye. While the yellow, orange and white flowers we selected caught one's attention, they did not do so to the extent that different-coloured foliage would have done and – crucially – not before one's eye had first come to rest on the view of the water.

Simplicity is normally the only way to achieve a sense of harmony. But in my experience, true simplicity is the hardest thing to achieve. Towards that end, every garden must have a single theme: one overridingly important feature which carries such weight that it binds the composition into one entity. Everything that is

done in the garden must be either subordinate to this idea or else eliminated. In my family's garden at Cloyne, the dry stone walls provided the cohesive factor. At the Villa Noailles the theme was water. Here, the theme was the view of the harbour.

Every garden, including one as informal as this, needs strong discipline. Accordingly, the view was framed with plants so as to emphasise the fact that the sea was the focal point one way and, conversely, that the house was the focal point when seen from the harbour. However, since this was an informal garden, it was important that the framing be suggested rather than emphatically stated.

Using bamboo supported by *Strelitzia nicolai* on one side and a large palm tree and *Strelitzia nicolai* on the other, I framed the reversible focal points by positioning these plants to imply an arch – rather like the proscenium arch in a theatre. In the theatre, a proscenium arch creates a seemingly mystical barrier between the audience and the stage. In fact, this barrier is neither mystical nor magical but depends for effect on the real or apparent shade falling between viewer and viewed. I wished the principle to work in precisely the same way here. The *audience* – in the garden – would stand in filtered light, the deepest band of shade occurring at the point of the arch; and the *stage* – or, in this case, the harbour – would stand in full sunlight as if drenched by arc lights. From this vantage point, the lit stage is given a heightened sense of reality. Such a perspective also creates the illusion that the illuminated object is closer than it actually is.

Looking the other way – from the harbour back towards the house – the proscenium arch works in reverse effect. The garden, bathed in filtered light, assumes an air of mystery when seen from a position of

ABOVE *Golden bamboo screens the neighbouring house and garden from view. By hiding the boundary fence, the bamboo gives the impression that the garden might be larger than it appears. The wooden path and steps lead down towards the harbour in a relaxed, meandering fashion.*

bright sunlight through a band of shade. And since the focal point is now darker than the vantage point, it has the illusion of being further away.

A strong focal point also implies an axial line, which was reinforced by a flight of simple wooden steps designed to pass through the jungle towards the harbour's edge. Such axial lines, real or implied, are important to informal gardens. And the wooden steps helped lead the eye towards the sea.

Since lawns are incompatible with jungles, we did not plant grass in the rainforest but used groundcover plants such as agapanthus, *Gardenia augusta* 'Radicans', clivia and hemerocallis instead. At the time, it was perceived to be quite a radical departure from normal gardening practice in Sydney. Unlike a lawn, which can be laid in a matter of hours to create an immediately pleasing effect, groundcover plants are prohibitively expensive to use in this way. The only thing to do is to plant them at sensible intervals and then wait for them to grow and cover the ground. This can take years, and it requires a special kind of client to have such patience.

In this garden, however, groundcover plants were essential for several reasons. Firstly, they enhanced the mood of a wild, untamed subtropical jungle, whereas large areas of lawn would have made the space seem docile in spirit. Secondly, planted in wide and bold drifts, the groundcover plants gave the scheme a sense of cohesion. They brought together our eclectic choice of trees and shrubs which, whilst creating a loose, monochromatic tapestry of green in themselves, nonetheless needed a unifying carpet. The intention was that these bold drifts of carpeting plants should further impel the eye down the slope towards the view of the sea.

Two decades later, this garden continues to sit comfortably on its site and has the sense of excitement I wished to create. Interestingly enough, I have recently designed a garden on a very similar site nearby. In fact, the two gardens are no more than a kilometre apart, and are within sight of each other. Here, on a level sandstone shelf several metres above the sea and overlaid with sandy soil, we have taken our cue from the existence of several endemic trees and used indigenous plants that once would have grown naturally on the site. These include *Angophora costata*, *Angophora hispida*, *Eucalyptus haemastoma*, *Banksia serrata*, *Banksia ericifolia*, *Allocasuarina distyla* and *Hakea teretifolia*.

There is no automatic watering system in this newer garden and so the plants thrive on a combination of rainfall and some sporadic watering with a hand-held hose. Certain parts of the garden are mixed with exotic plants from dry habitats such as succulents – particularly aloes – and one senses a gratifying harmony between the unmulched sandy soil and the character of the plants growing in it.

It is very hard to define in a precise, scientific way all the components that made my first Sydney garden what it is, since an undercurrent of often subconscious emotion also played a role. The interior designer, Leslie Walford, gathering a group of house painters around him in a bedroom he was decorating, once said, 'Now, on these walls, I see freshly gathered hay . . .'

'Jeez, Mr Walford,' one of the painters said incredulously. 'What colour is that?'

'It's not a colour. It's a mood. Just do it.'

And at times, I must confess, I am tempted to trust my instinct – sharpened by experience – and not overly analyse my motives. I just do it.

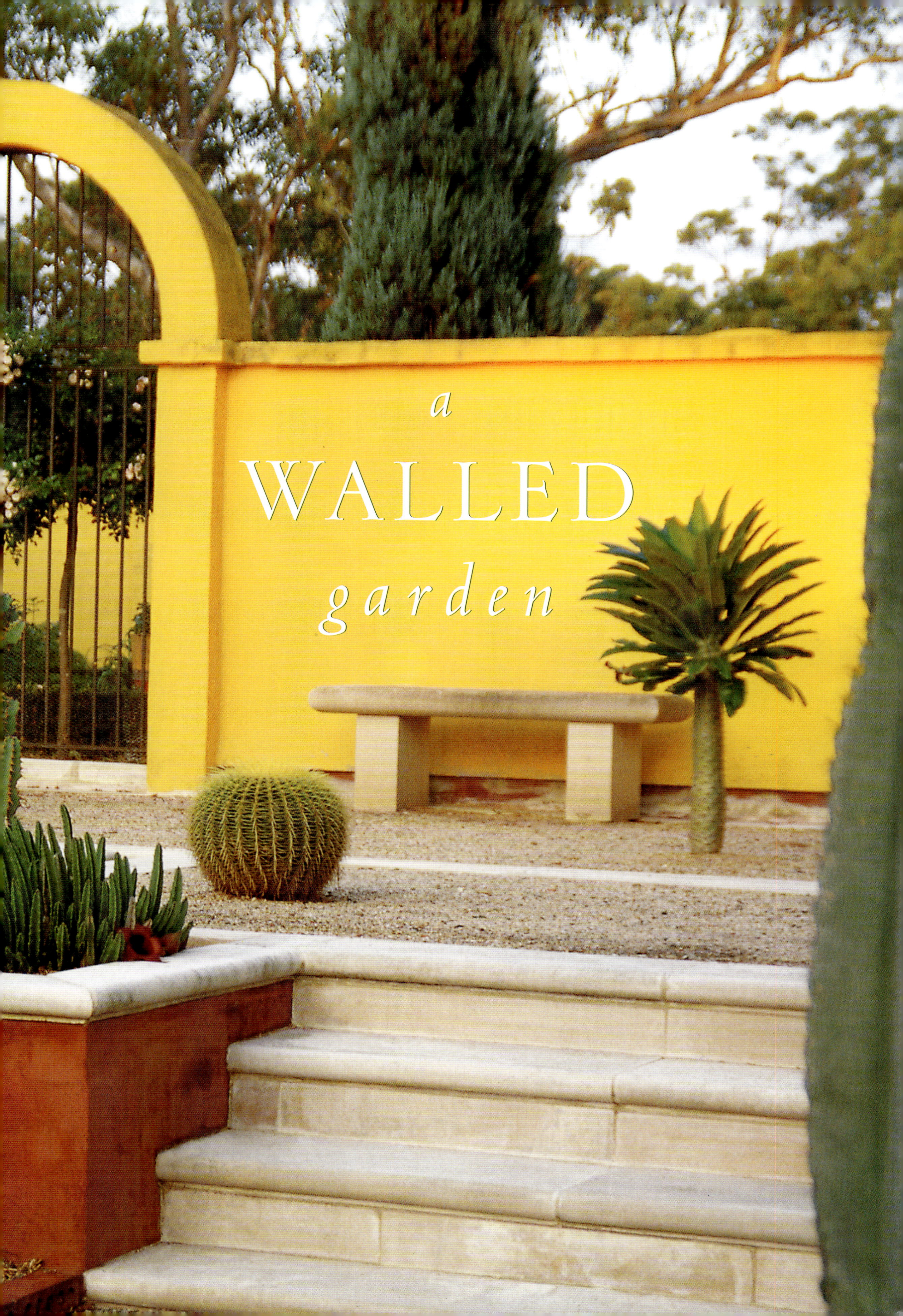
a
WALLED
garden

I n 1978 I was contacted by Gunther and Gitta Rembel, who owned two hectares of virgin bushland to the northwest of Dural, on the outskirts of Sydney. They wanted me to see the land and give them ideas for the garden before they finalised the design of their house. From a landscape designer's perspective, this is a wise move. I spent an entire Sunday with the Rembels looking at the site of their future house.

Gunther and Gitta had originally come to Australia from East Germany. They were clearly awed by the beauty of the land and, endearingly, spoke to me in hushed voices as if we were in a cathedral. It was indeed a remarkable place. The top half of their property was relatively level, while the bottom half fell steeply away, over a series of sandstone cliffs, to a gully some fifty metres below. A forest of trees clambered up this slope – a mixture of red and yellow bloodwoods, *Angophora costata*, *Angophora hispida*, black she-oaks, *Banksia serrata*, *Lambertia formosa* and flax wattle. Here and there were also occasional scribbly bark gum trees.

As you emerged onto the flat terrain above, these gum trees with their white scribbled-upon trunks took over, creating an interesting open woodland that reflected the subtle change in habitat. To the west were views through the forest to the Blue Mountains, and despite being on the outskirts of Sydney not a single sign of humanity could be discerned. It was breathtakingly beautiful.

On the level land, close to the entrance from the road and surrounded by the grove of scribbly bark gum trees, was a huge expanse of flat sandstone. Here, Gunther and Gitta said they would build their house, because in doing so they would have to fell only one tree. I agreed with them. But the Rembels also wanted to have a swimming pool, a vegetable garden, an orchard of citrus trees, a tennis court and a lawn on which to play games. I was perplexed. How, I asked, could we possibly reconcile this with the bush? That's why we need your advice, they replied. My conscience told me that I should be advising them not to have any garden – that the garden was already there in the bushland that made up this spectacular site.

As the day progressed, however, a solution occurred to me. If the Rembels were prepared to raise their garden above the natural level of the bush – to divorce it from the virgin soil – and to enclose it within walls, then a sharp contrast could be created between the native vegetation and the *humanised* landscape of the garden. Apart from a few stepping stones wending their way through it, the bush beyond the proposed walls of the gardens would remain completely untouched. The garden, therefore, would be as alien to the natural site as the house itself. Only by physically dividing the natural bush from the garden did I feel that the two had a chance to coexist happily.

After this, the details fell into place as if of their own volition, and I spent the rest of the afternoon perched on a sandstone boulder, committing them to paper. The plans, while not drawn to scale, gave the precise measurements of the complex of gardens that I envisaged.

This garden complex would sit primarily on the northern side of the house as dictated by the terrain. It would consist of a succession of gardens, each on a large level terrace. These terraces would be held in place by brick walls that had been 'bagged', or lightly rendered, to soften their impact. In fact, the retaining walls of the garden could be built as part of the house itself, literally forming a series of outdoor rooms.

From the doors of the kitchen you would walk down some wide steps into the swimming-pool garden, which would stand some three metres above the existing flat sandstone rocks. The design of this garden terrace would be very simple with the swimming pool, a simple rectangle, resting in the centre. Around the edges would be rectilinear garden beds planted with subtropical plants such as palms, gardenias, *Cestrum nocturnum* and *Phoenix roebelenii*. These plants would be protected to the north and east by tall rendered brick walls, and to the west by panels of glass, giving spectacular views through the indigenous forest onto the Blue Mountains.

On the eastern side of the swimming-pool garden, a gate in the brick wall would lead you two steps down to the next terrace. A change of level, no matter how small, always helps to emphasise the fact that you are going from one *world* into another. In this case, you would enter a long arbour, made of slender metal arches, completely covered in wisteria. The arbour would be flanked on its left by a citrus orchard — with orange, lemon, tangelo and grapefruit trees — planted in formal rows on a wide, raised lawn. On the far side of this grove, in keeping with the basic theme of the garden, the retaining wall would fall straight down onto the sandstone rocks below.

At the end of the wisteria arbour, the path would turn left to intersect with the central gate of the proposed tennis court. The tennis court would be constructed at a lower level again to the arbour and citrus garden. At its eastern end there would be a raised stage on which people could sit and watch the game.

On reaching the central gate that led into the tennis court, the path would make a right-angled turn and, flanking the lower half of the court, reach the entrance to the vegetable garden. Like the swimming-pool garden, the vegetable garden would be enclosed within tall rendered walls. It would be higher than the tennis court, and this change of level once again would serve to disassociate one part of the garden from the other. The reason for the high walls in the vegetable garden was not so much to exclude the wind, but to create the mysterious mood and sense of inviolable privacy that a walled garden can give. I had run out of time, however, to give details of the layout of the vegetable garden.

Handing over my sketches at the end of the day, I was surprised by the lack of any resistance to this indulgent garden of pure fantasy. Gunther and Gitta simply agreed with the suggestions and said they would telephone me if they needed any more advice. That evening, however, I felt some misgivings about presenting such extravagant plans, involving so much onerous work and expense, to people who were probably too kind

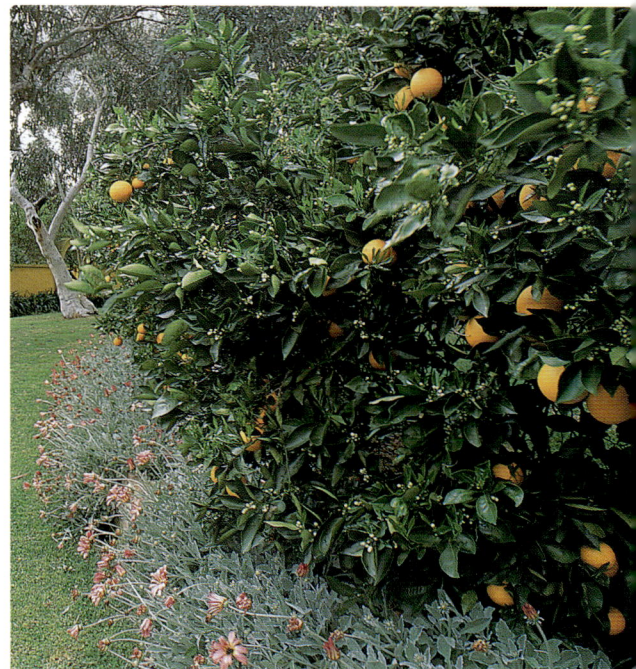

PREVIOUS PAGES *At the end of the formal cactus and succulent garden is a raised stage overlooking the entire garden. Seen through the grille in the arch is the vegetable garden.*
TOP *The scribbly bark gum tree,* Eucalyptus haemastoma, *is, as its name suggests, covered with interesting squiggly hieroglyphics.*
ABOVE Gazania *is a good groundcover plant for the base of citrus trees as its foliage creates a contrast — of both texture and colour — with the green shiny leaves above.*

[27]

to tell me that I had wasted their entire day. It didn't surprise me not to hear from them.

Two years later, out of the blue, came a call from the Rembels. Did I remember them? Would I come and see them again in Dural and advise them on the next stage?

The garden that greeted my eyes astounded me. In all my years of making gardens I have never been quite so surprised. The Rembels had carried out my advice precisely. The retaining walls were at the prescribed height above the bushland, creating the dichotomy I had hoped for. The swimming pool was protected from the westerly winds by glass panels and surrounded by the subtropical trees and shrubs I had recommended, including palms, bananas, gardenias and jasmine. The citrus orchard, too, had been planted just as I had imagined. Even more amazing was that Gunther, with the help of his brother, Manfred, had done much of the construction of both the house and the garden himself at weekends and, quite often, under arc lamps on weeknights after work. It was an astounding achievement.

As I had envisaged – but had not dared hope – Gunther and Manfred had laid the foundations for the house and the garden's outdoor rooms at the same time. They had then brought in professional bricklayers to construct the walls. On reaching the site on their first morning, the brickies looked dubiously at the intricate system of foundations. 'What are you building here, mate?' one asked. 'A supermarket or something?'

The following year, Gunther and Gitta asked me to design the detail of the vegetable garden. The design was a logical geometric continuation of the existing complex of gardens, and could not have been simpler. The garden would be laid out in a formal fashion like a French *potager*, quartered by brick paved paths. Each quarter would contain four small garden beds in which to grow vegetables or flowers.

The two principal paths that divided the garden would be one and a half metres wide. These dimensions were important as they represented the minimum width enabling two people to walk abreast of each other. Gardens are places in which to relax, and the scale of paths and other architectural features should reflect this. The garden's subsidiary paths, however, which dissected each quarter into smaller beds, would be considerably narrower.

Attention also needed to be paid to the design of the garden's two principal axes. While the main axis would end in a wooden garden seat, placed against the wall, the cross axis would direct the eye to the west, through an arch in the garden wall, and onto the stage at the end of the tennis court. Apart from this single view of the outside world, the garden would be completely introspective. To the east, it would focus on a

gargoyle mounted on the wall with a semicircular pond below, and at its centre would lie a circular pond with a jet of water.

The design of the garden was, in large part, influenced by my reading about gardens in the river valleys of the Tigris and Euphrates. These gardens – some of the earliest ever made – were designed as places in which one could not only grow vegetables and flowers but relax. Beyond all practical considerations they were symbolic and, since water is the source of all life, water took its place in the centre of the gardens. To create added drama, we intended to plant an Italian cypress in each corner of the garden where they would act as four huge exclamation marks. But realising that these trees would quickly become too large and dwarf the comparatively small enclosure, we planted *Juniperus virginiana* 'Skyrocket' instead.

Two years later the vegetable garden was finished, and we were ready to discuss the lawn that the Rembels wished to have on the south side of the house, away from our succession of gardens *enfilade*. Lawns rarely accord well with the Australian bush and, in particular, with forests of eucalypts. To begin with, eucalypts are greedy and seize much of the moisture and nutrients near the surface of the soil, leaving lawns looking threadbare. Furthermore, lawns are a northern European invention, suited to the temperate climates from which they originally came. This is not to say that in the right context they cannot be hugely successful in both subtropical and tropical climates. But in dryer climates there is something decidedly unconvincing about lawns unless handled in a special way. Certainly to have an emerald-green lawn that gradually petered out into a natural scribbly bark forest standing on Hawkesbury sandstone would have looked ridiculous.

Once again, I decided to follow our theme of separating the man-made garden from the natural bushland by designing a serpentine retaining wall, approximately one metre high, which insinuated its way through the bush echoing the shapes of the surrounding sandstone boulders. The lawn, like the rest of the garden, thus belonged to a different world – in both a practical and a symbolic sense – and its emerald-green colour coexisted with the bush only because the contrast was so strongly reinforced.

The complex of gardens was now almost complete, but in the middle of the formal gardens the space

ABOVE *The swimming-pool garden is planted with subtropical plants such as palms, dracaenas, banana trees and gardenias. It is a walled enclosure, standing some three metres above the forest, which differentiates between the artificial world and the real world beyond the garden.*

for the tennis court stood vacant and rather ugly. I kept in regular contact with the Rembels, but for the next ten years we simply watched the existing gardens grow. And, as time passed, we almost became used to the sandy, empty tennis court site. Then in 1995, Gunther and Gitta announced that they didn't want a tennis court after all. They were so busy working in the garden during their spare time, when would they find time to play? What, they asked, could we do with the vacant site? Could we perhaps do something unusual?

I had long wished to design a formal cactus and succulent garden – something I have never seen anywhere in the world – and suggested this idea to the Rembels. I have often wondered why people in most parts of Australia don't grow more succulent and cactus plants. After all, they are used a great deal in similar climates in places such as California, Texas and the Mediterranean countries.

Just as in the vegetable garden, a circular pond was placed in the centre of the cactus garden, only this time the pond was to be much larger. Because the stark contrast between water and the dry conditions required to grow cacti and succulents created an interesting tension, both a chadar, or water chute, and a rill were added. In the Mogul gardens of northern India and Pakistan, the chadar is used as a symbolic waterfall, cooling the air with tumbling water and refreshing one's spirit with its sound. The rill, of course, symbolises a river. The more I worked with these ideas, the more they appealed to me. And in the end this garden became, more than anything else, a water garden: a place in which water is celebrated as a rare and prized possession.

Like the Moors and the Moguls, I wanted the thread of water in the garden to be like the unfolding plot of a story being told out loud. Water enters the garden through identical jets in two rectangular ponds on opposite sides of the raised stage, which is not unlike the stage of a theatre. From each of these, two small canals merge into a single rill at the stage's centre, before changing direction towards the water chute. After tumbling down the water chute, the rill carries the water towards the large circular pond before disappearing beneath the path. The water then apparently re-emerges through a tall jet in the middle of the central pond. For practical reasons, the two systems of water – that of the rill and that of the pond – are in reality quite independent of each other.

In designing the layout of the garden beds and paths I created a symmetrical scheme using zigzags and acute angles far more than I have ever before been tempted to do. Whenever I have seen them in their native state in Mexico and Arizona, the silhouette of large cactus plants against the sky always gives me a certain thrill of excitement. Similarly, the surrounding hills and rocky outcrops on the desert floor are often jagged rather than soft and rounded. In order to re-create some of this harshness and tension, at least in a symbolic way, I decided to make the geometry so acute as to be almost uncomfortable. It also provided garden beds that extended out into the paths like peninsulas. On these we placed some of the largest cacti for optimum effect.

The view back towards the house from this desert garden always gives me pleasure. From this perspective, the cacti and succulents, isolated once again by a retaining wall, can be seen in conjunction with the moisture-loving citrus garden. Such a view from artificial desert to artificial oasis also creates a fascinating tension. It is just the same as the precise line demarcating the desert from the irrigated citrus orchards that one sees when approaching Phoenix, Arizona, by air.

The only part of the cactus and succulent garden that is not strictly symmetrical is its southwest corner. Here, unexpectedly, is a sunken garden, a place in which to sit and look up at the plants in the surrounding garden beds. It is also a place to have dinner on summer evenings, or lunch during cooler months.

One of the unexpected pleasures of the Rembel's garden for me is the contribution made by one of Gunther and Gitta's sons, Ralph, who is an interior designer. Under his direction, the colours of both the house and the garden walls were changed. Whereas I was content with either bagged or white walls as a foil for the foliage of the plants, Ralph painted them stark earthen colours with a boldness worthy of the Mexican architect, Luis Barragán. This change of colour has made an important contribution to the garden. It struck me at the time as being entirely logical and provoked me into seeing the garden in a more dynamic way. In retrospect, it was one of several factors that inspired me to recommend, and then design, the cactus and succulent garden.

The Rembels' garden plays with contrasting habitats more than any other garden I have designed. Divorcing these different habitats, both laterally and vertically, has meant that interesting games can be played without compromising the garden's integrity within the context of the natural landscape. Each outdoor room has its own sense of place independent of that of its neighbour.

ABOVE *The planting on this gravel-covered stage is sparse and sculptural, adding to the surreality of the scheme. The rounded shapes of* Echinocactus grusonii *contrast with the upright forms of* Pachypodium lamerei.

The crucial issue here is that the outdoor rooms are simply that: rooms that form part of the house. And although it might appear otherwise, the complex of gardens that we have created is a celebration of the Australian bush in the same indirect way that the gardens of the Alhambra are a celebration of the wild Andulusian landscape beyond the confines of its walls. What we have created is an extension of the house and a frame through which the real world — the native bushland — can be seen and enjoyed.

a WATERFALL garden

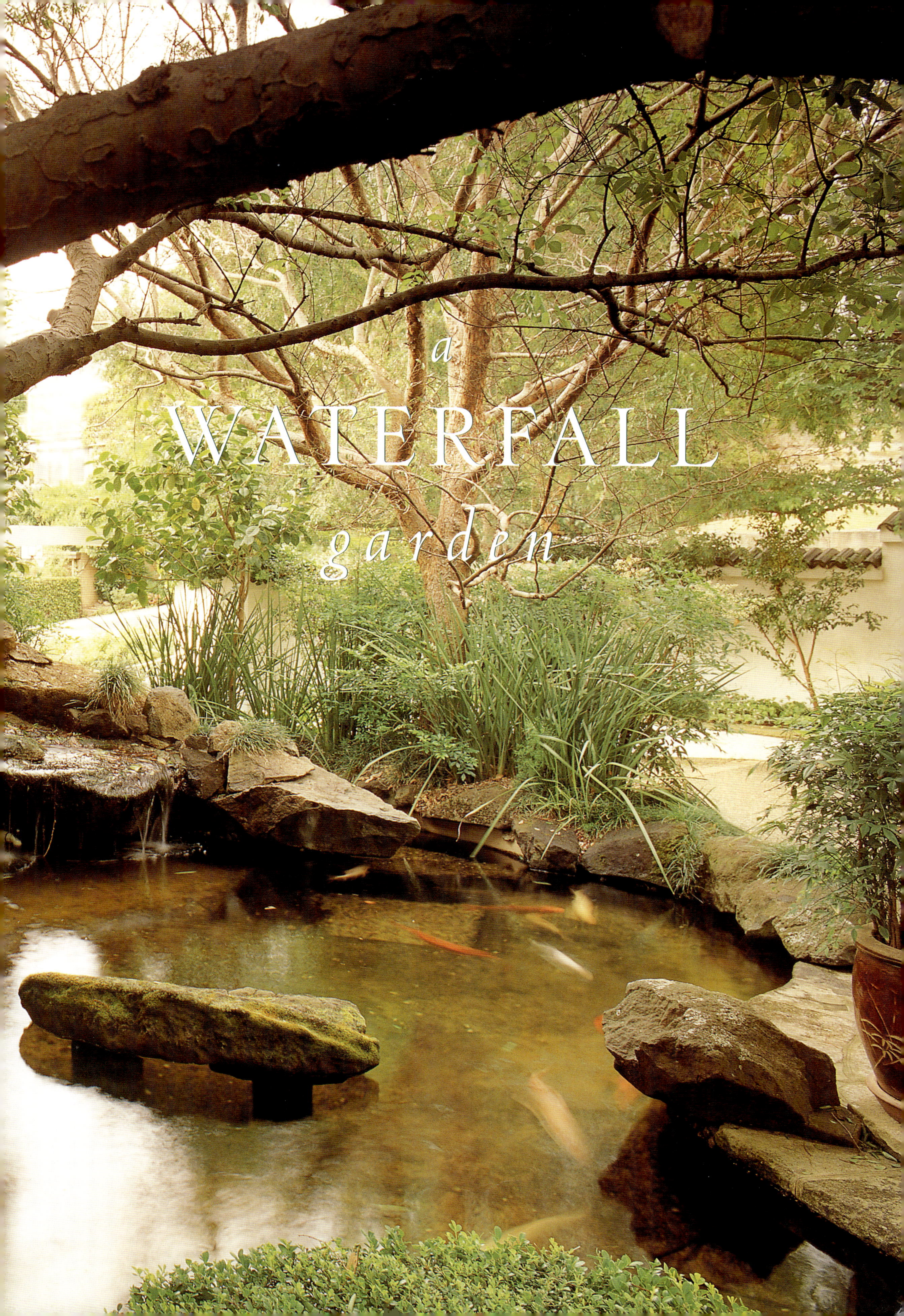

*I*n the late 1970s an architect, Andrew Briger, asked me to design a small garden for a house built in the 1920s, which he was remodelling for a client. Initially the client asked me to design a Japanese garden for this site in Vaucluse, Sydney, but I felt unqualified to do it. Japanese gardens derive their integrity from a profound understanding of Zen Buddhism. Without that knowledge, which it is said must be inculcated from early childhood to be truly understood, it is impossible to design such gardens other than in the most rudimentary fashion.

Certainly those so-called Zen gardens that were created by American landscape designers in California earlier in the twentieth century have an intrinsic Disneyland quality about them. Nevertheless, while saying that I could not design a Japanese garden, I did say that I could do one that was loosely Japanese in spirit.

The tapered site on which I was to make this garden sloped up from the street, becoming progressively wider as it approached the garage and house. At that point, it was approximately twelve metres wide by twenty metres long. But because a double garage protruded into this space, much of the available area was necessarily taken up with the driveway and the parking of cars. The only area remaining in which to create a garden was opposite the garage on the upper right-hand side of the site. The terrain here was level, and led directly to the front door of the house.

I felt that the best use of this small space was to make a garden that was as private and as enclosed as possible, hiding the wide expanses of paved drive as well as the street beyond. Such arid and sterile spaces are alienating to the spirit, no matter how fleeting and subconscious their effect might be. This garden needed to be an antidote to that. And as the space was constrained and overlooked by its neighbours, it would not be a garden in which one could sit and relax. Rather it would be a garden to be enjoyed whilst coming and going from the front door; a place in which one might find momentary refreshment.

Perhaps the greatest asset any garden can have is water, its sight and sound inducing a sense of calm and wellbeing. Indeed, research suggests that breaking water – cascades, fountains and the surf – produces positive ions, and it is their presence in the air that temporarily alters the chemistry of the brain and leads to a sense of tranquillity. Because of the powerful, restorative effect of falling water – and keeping in mind the Japanese spirit of the garden – I designed a waterfall as the main feature of the garden.

Waterfalls, however, are not a natural feature of Vaucluse. The few streams that once existed, before being buried beneath suburbia, were too modest to create such cascades, except as a result of occasional thunderstorms. The anomaly did not concern me unduly. This was to be a courtyard garden surrounded by walls on three sides and a driveway on the fourth. It was to be introspective, and hence was not being designed in relation to any indigenous landscape.

Nevertheless, in order to create some kind of rapport with the natural surroundings that once existed,

I decided to construct the waterfall from indigenous sandstone. I had hoped to find local Hawkesbury sandstone, so as to be as true to the site as possible, but these boulders proved impossible to find. After much searching, we finally located some sandstone boulders from Gundagai, some five hundred kilometres away, that were all but indistinguishable from those of the Sydney region.

I felt that the waterfall and its surrounding pond needed to be made as large as possible, and that we should stage-manage an element of surprise. Apart from the obvious sound of falling water, I wanted there to be no hint of the existence of so much water in such a small space until one actually entered that part of the garden. The intention was that the visitor, by way of an oblique path, should already have passed from the drive into a space enclosed by plants before seeing the waterfall. Moreover, just as the waterfall was to be the last thing that visitors saw on entering the garden, so should it be the first thing they saw upon leaving the house. And so it was placed diagonally opposite the front door, in the southeastern corner of the enclosure.

Whilst being close to any waterfall is refreshing and invigorating, this experience is magnified when one is in a small space, surrounded by plants. To contain the sense of coolness and calm given by the waterfall, I designed two garden beds. The first would extend from the front door of the house, and run down the windowless garage wall. The second — having left enough space for the oblique path leading into the garden — would actually enclose the garden on its southern side, hiding and separating it from the sloping drive.

In order for this second bed to perform its task of concealing the waterfall from the drive, it needed to be raised above ground level. And in keeping with the Japanese mood of the garden, the change in elevation had to be achieved in a relatively informal manner. The best way to do it would be to use the same sandstone

PREVIOUS PAGES *Because of the magic of falling water in a confined space, and in keeping with the Japanese spirit of the garden, a waterfall was designed as the garden's main feature.* BELOW *The garden was designed to be the last thing seen on approaching the house via the path on the left-hand side of the picture, and the first thing seen on leaving.*

being used for the waterfall. Since the waterfall would sit immediately behind this bed, it would naturally form part of it.

Because the garden and waterfall faced southeast, they received sunlight only in the morning. This was a bonus as the plants I wanted to use would, in general, prefer a shady southerly aspect to a sunny northerly one. Most of them were originally from Asia, but were plants that thrived in Sydney.

I began with trees, planting several semi-mature Chinese elms, *Ulmus parvifolia*. They created an overhead canopy, giving further shade to the courtyard. Beneath these trees were planted several shrubs of *Camellia japonica* and *Camellia sasanqua* – both natives of Japan – for autumn, winter and spring flowers, along with various azaleas. For scent during the summer months I used two natives of China, *Gardenia jasminoides* 'Florida' and star jasmine, *Trachelospermum jasminoides*. I also used a number of ferns, including Australian tree ferns, which thrived in the cool, moist air.

At first glance, it may seem a drastically simple choice of plants, but I didn't want the planting to upstage the drama of the waterfall. One of the hardest tasks as a landscape gardener can be persuading clients to exercise restraint in their planting schemes. But such discipline is important. It often happens that plants which are not spectacular in themselves come into their own when contrasted with neighbouring plants. Once again, what underpins this garden and gives it a certain authority is the fact that this combination of plants is ecologically compatible.

During the garden's construction a large mobile crane was hired to lift the sandstone boulders over electricity cables and onto the site. We were fortunate in that the operator of the crane had a calm nature alloyed with infinite patience. To ensure that the waterfall looked as natural as possible, I followed no preconceived plan but responded purely to the shape and size of the boulders and to the feel of the site in deciding where each should go. All day long I tried dozens of possibilities with different boulders, slowly building up the waterfall stone by stone. No pressure was placed upon me to work any faster. The noise of machinery was deafening, and yet the atmosphere was serene. As a result the waterfall, completed in early 1980, is something I can look upon today with satisfaction.

As originally promised, the garden has quite a Japanese feeling, but these qualities are suggested rather than stated. What is interesting – indeed flattering – is that the present owners of this garden are Japanese and they have maintained it well without making changes to the original design.

PREVIOUS PAGES *There are almost twenty carp in the pond and they give this purposely subdued garden surges of movement and colour in a way that flowers cannot.* OPPOSITE *This Port Jackson fig is a most welcome intruder into the garden – until it reaches such a size that it will physically threaten the structure of the waterfall.*

a

WOODLAND

garden

My first sight of the garden in Bloomfield Hills, Michigan, on which I was to spend an average of more than two months a year for the next twelve years, and which was to become one of the most important gardens of my career, was not so prepossessing. Its drive was paved with black asphalt and the yew topiaries planted in the entrance courtyard were in the Californian Château style. Its large lawns were peppered with blue conifers that looked like Christmas trees running riot in the wrong season. I felt immediately that much would need to be swept away before any start could be made on creating an attractive garden.

Despite this, the site had good bones. It was just over four hectares in size and shaped like an open fan. One entered from the public road at the base of the fan and proceeded along the drive to the two-storeyed house, which was sited in the middle of the grounds. Because it was so large and broad, the house blocked most views of the garden beyond. The ground between the entrance gate and the house was relatively level, but just beyond the house the site sloped downhill quite steeply before levelling out again at its broadly arced perimeter. The broad arc, representing the top of the fan, was created by a delightful, slightly meandering, tree-lined road, beyond which were school playing fields set amongst woods, and a small stream.

This topography meant that there were two distinct areas to be landscaped. The first was the level land on the northern side of the garden, which extended from the main entrance to the house, and which was traversed on one side by the semicircular drive. The second area was the broader wedge of the fan on the southern side of the house with its view across the valley. On closer acquaintance, however, I realised that on the eastern side of the broad wedge, the end of the fan tilted away from the house on a convex slope creating a third area which, because it was so separate from the house and the rest of the garden, had its own special air of mystery. Because of this I felt the site of the garden had great potential.

Over dinner that first night in their temporary apartment, I discussed the garden with my clients, summoning up the courage to tell them that any worthwhile design would necessitate starting from scratch. Fortunately they agreed. The house, which had been originally constructed in the 1950s, would also be gutted to a shell and, over the next nine months, rebuilt. William Hodgins of Boston would be the interior designer of the house, except for the bathrooms, which were to be the responsibility of the French interior designer, Andrée Putman. It was a most distinguished team to be working with.

PREVIOUS PAGES *A sugar maple leans towards the road at the height of autumn. Being one of several mature indigenous trees on the property, it indicated the way in which this garden might be developed.* OPPOSITE *Its age, association with the history of the garden, and glorious beauty when in flower gives this very old crab-apple tree special significance in this native, woodland garden.*

[48]

My clients' intention was to make their house as unstylised as possible, thereby giving it an integrity it currently lacked. We were on the same wavelength. This young couple, both of whom were still in their twenties and full of infectious enthusiasm, were clearly perfectionists. They wanted exciting ideas and, at the same time, expected them to be executed with an eye for detail.

By exploring the neighbourhood, I learnt that the site of the garden would once have been a mixed forest of red oak, sugar maples, sassafras and white pine. In the grounds of neighbouring Cranbrook School, American plane trees or sycamores, *Platanus occidentalis*, still thrived, as in the days when the only thoroughfares through these valleys were Indian trails. The strongest single spark giving a clue to the original character of the place was the view onto these stands of trees. Seeming to reach towards the sky, sycamores have a flaky white, almost ghost-like bark which glows eerily in the evening light. And their boles in old age can be so large and hollow that, according to old-timers in rural Ohio, 'a calf could get itself hid inside'.

Discussing these unique qualities with my clients on that first day, we decided that the principal, unifying theme of the garden would be indigenous trees planted in an informal, miniature parkland setting. It would be an idealised romantic landscape, in which trees native to southeastern Michigan would not only frame the house but also create interesting views from it. The guiding principle was to create a landscape that the Indians who once inhabited these valleys might recognise as having a certain integrity.

In keeping with this, trees would be planted to give a sense of movement and to hide the garden's boundaries as far as possible. Densely planted copses of unseen – and therefore indeterminate – depth would imitate nature, casting degrees of shade and constantly conditioning and reconditioning the light to create an air of mystery. From their darkest centres these small woods would unfurl like miniature emerging galaxies before gradually disintegrating, casting clear certain random specimens to stand in solitary isolation on the lawn. As you walked through the garden, views would compose and recompose, each element linked to the whole.

This was little different in principle from the English landscape garden of the eighteenth century. But as it eventuated, the garden in Bloomfield Hills proved to be one of the first I designed in the style I consider my own. Whereas my first priority, like that of the eighteenth-century designers, was to link the garden to its surroundings and site, and for this informal landscape to become the *field* of the garden, I also added formal elements to blend with the informal.

In all of the gardens he designed, Capability Brown brought his informal plantations of trees from the horizon right up to the house, sweeping away anything he considered contradictory. Notwithstanding my admiration for his work, I find such single-mindedness undesirable. At Longleat in Wiltshire, for instance, I would have preferred Capability Brown to have left untouched the formal parterres around the house, which were designed by London and Wise in the seventeenth century. A large, symmetrical house like Longleat is in itself an extremely formal element in the landscape. In order to ease the house smoothly into its pastoral setting, the first step should be a degree of discreet formality close to the house. By discreet formality I mean that it should help to lead the eye into the view rather than demand undue attention in the foreground.

In the garden in Bloomfield Hills, I decided that formality would play a limited role. The first concern, however, was to resolve any jarring elements that impinged on my plans for an informal parkland garden. These elements were the sight of the three neighbouring houses, all designed in vastly different architectural styles; the exotic trees surrounding their gardens; and the sight and sound of traffic passing along the road. All would have to either be blocked from view or else have their presence diminished, in order to create the desired effect.

The paradox was that in order to give this garden a sense of belonging to the locality which is Bloomfield Hills, it would have to be cut off from at least two-thirds of its present surroundings. Apart from the views along its southern boundary, this garden would be necessarily introspective.

In those days in America's garden suburbs, it was not fashionable to cut off a garden from its neighbour or the road. Expansive, seemingly never-ending lawns were shared by everyone who lived on the block. If America ever espoused communist principals in any broad fashion, then it certainly did so with suburban lawns. In many instances the only way you could tell where one garden ended and the other began was if the lawn-mowers of the various owners had left a different pattern on the grass. To me it was absurd that a neo-Tudor house, for example, should share the same lawn and so appear to be part of the same landscape as the ranch-style bungalow next door. The only way that any of these gardens could hope to achieve integrity would be to enclose them in their own spaces.

In January 1984 I returned to Detroit, and after various lengthy consultations with my clients I designed a stone wall that represented our declaration of independence from the communal front lawn. The use of stone would give a sense of permanence to the garden. A stone wall some-how demonstrates a clear commitment to a particular place by those who build it. Furthermore, it lends a sense of occasion to daily arrivals and departures.

The valleys of Bloomfield Hills are full of round granite stones left long ago as moraine by retreating glaciers. By using this stone, the wall would be something that grew out of the land on which it was built. It belonged to the site far more than the endless lawns. Nevertheless, had we laid the football-sized stones as they were found, the effect would have been too rustic. The answer was to split them, although not by machine. We didn't want the result to resemble the stone veneer wall of a local bank. Instead, we had the stones split by hand, a job that kept one man gainfully employed all winter. The resulting wall gave the garden a discernible sense of place. At the same time, it was the first formal element introduced to the garden: a six-foot-high streak of symmetry, cutting through what eventually would be an informal woodland.

In the end, we also needed to plant hedges on both sides of the garden in order to create the right degree of remoteness from the neigh-bouring houses. Because the hedges were planted in straight lines and clipped, another formal element was introduced. Such an exotic concept could surely support an exotic plant, and so I used very large yew plants, *Taxus* × *hicksii*.

When it was completed in the summer of 1984, the wall looked very new and stark, despite the fact that behind it stood a venerable American elm of great age, as well as a few other smaller trees of interest. It was important to 'clothe' it as quickly as possible. Extraordinarily, the first attempts to establish that toughest of all imaginable plants, ivy, did not succeed. The ivy succumbed in the first winter. Later, when it finally did grow, it was by painfully slow increments.

ABOVE *When creating compositions with deciduous trees, one of the most important considerations is the way in which their foliage will modulate the spring, summer and autumn light.*

The plant that did best of all was the deciduous climbing hydrangea, *Hydrangea petiolaris*, which has the advantage of clinging by itself. For a number of years, I planted several 'New Dawn' roses on the wall. These, too, thrived, and each summer the granite would be smothered in flowers. But as the surrounding trees grew, the roses were gradually shaded out of existence. A number of clematis did surprisingly well, in spite of Michigan's bitterly cold winters, and Dutchman's pipe, *Aristolochia macrophylla*, with its large heart-shaped leaves, took happily to the shadiest parts of the wall where I feared nothing at all would survive.

Simply clothing the wall in climbing plants was not enough to create the air of mystery and the feeling of permanency I wanted. The twenty-foot-wide lawn that ran between the wall and the road needed trees. More specifically, to create a strong and simple effect it needed one type of tree and this, of course, had to be a native of Michigan. To find such a tree, Chuck Irish, a third-generation tree surgeon, and I flew to Chicago where we searched several nurseries for something special. Finally, we stumbled across a copse of Ohio sweet buckeyes, *Aesculus glabra*. These are medium-sized trees, smaller than but similar to horse chestnuts, and also natives of Michigan. I was entranced by the shape and colour of their leaves, and the effect they have on natural sunlight when planted as a copse.

In the United States, perhaps more than in any other country in the world, plants go in and out of fashion — in itself a bizarre concept — and

PREVIOUS PAGES *This copse of thirty-one birch trees not only enhances the garden's woodland mood, but also partially screens the house from the lower part of the garden.* OPPOSITE *At the entrance to the garden a two-metre-high wall was designed to give a sense of privacy. To convey the woodland feel of the garden, a lawn was made on which was planted a copse of Ohio sweet buckeyes.* ABOVE *In spring this small group of zumi crab-apple trees is covered with a froth of bright white flowers, and in early summer the green foliage conditions the light in a most seductive way.*

[55]

Ohio sweet buckeyes were not *in* at that particular moment. Consequently, the trees we'd discovered were not really for sale, and not for the first time I was considered eccentric in wanting to buy eight of them. Nevertheless, when finally planted at the entrance, they immediately softened the wall and created the woodland effect we desired.

We had decided against having a gate on the wall since this would send the wrong message and make the garden seem like a fortress. However, by densely planting trees in the first half of the lawn that lay between the wall and the house, we could – since the drive was semi-circular in shape – block out the sight of the house from the road and also reduce the occasional traffic noise. Once fully grown, the trees that we planted on both sides of the newly gravelled drive would touch overhead. Those driving to the house would thus go from the sunlight of the road into the dappled light of the buckeyes, before passing through the stone wall into a relatively shady tunnel of enveloping foliage. A slight turn in the drive, and the house and entrance courtyard, seen across a wide expanse of almost empty lawn, would be framed by the trees before you finally emerged into full sunlight again. Such dynamic experiences of composition and recomposition – of compression and decompression – are what interesting landscape design is all about.

We had begun planting native Michigan trees in the garden from my first visit to Detroit. With the intention of also screening the neighbouring houses and their gardens, we planted a tight little grove of white pine, *Pinus strobus*, the state tree of Michigan. We also planted another conifer, the hemlock, *Tsuga canadensis*. In general, and with notable exceptions, I am not a great fan of conifers. Their shade is usually deep and potentially mournful, and it is not for nothing that André le Nôtre and Capability Brown used them sparingly, and only when the creation of such heavy moods was indicated. Capability Brown's favourite conifer was probably the Cedar of Lebanon. He used this, firstly, for its exotic silhouette – one that creates a mood which is anything but mournful; secondly, because it offers such a strong contrast in summer to deciduous trees; and finally, for its undoubted importance during winter months when the deciduous trees are leafless.

In a climate such as Detroit's, where snow is liable to lie on the ground for weeks, a landscape composed solely of deciduous trees is remarkably unsettling. The overcast sky and the snow-covered ground and branches merge into one, and everything seems to dissolve into the atmosphere. Such a light and insubstantial landscape can depress those who live in it. The effect of conifers is to anchor the sky to the ground and to create static points of reference during the winter months.

For this reason, as well as for the practical purpose of ensuring privacy for twelve months of the year, we used a comparatively large number of conifers between the stone wall and the house. Seen from the house, these hemlocks and white pines form a backdrop for the interesting, deciduous trees in the garden's foreground, and also create a sharp contrast in the garden. Perhaps the two great advantages of the conifers' dark-green foliage is that it creates an ideal foil for deciduous trees that flower in spring, and the foliage of which changes colour in autumn.

A deciduous native tree that appealed to me instantly for its distinctly American character was the shagbark hickory, *Carya ovata*. As its name suggests, this tree has rough bark that constantly peels off the trunk in long strips. The texture of the trunk, the shape and colour of the leaves, and the way that these leaves condition the light below the tree, encouraged me to plant a group of four.

We also planted copses of ironwoods, *Ostrya virginiana*, and Indian bean trees, *Catalpa speciosa*. The catalpas, with their large heart-shaped leaves and slender drooping beans, are for me the most American-looking of trees. In the books we had as children, *Johnny Appleseed* and *Hiawatha*, you could make out trees similar to these in the background of some of the pictures. The nurserymen were appalled. No one in their right mind would plant trees like the catalpa in a garden. Their constantly falling beans results in a state of almost perpetual litter on the ground below, making them the untidiest of all known trees. From my point of view, this was actually one of their most attractive points. Happily, my clients agreed.

They were less sympathetic when I planted a copse of ten very young, closely spaced sassafras trees. *Sassafras albidum* is one of the most dramatic of all autumn colouring trees, but cannot be transplanted as anything but a sapling. The sight of so many small trees in the garden caused irritation. Matters were not improved when only one tree survived the first winter. Once the dead trees had been replaced the following year, however, all survived and grew quickly. Their large, attractively lobed leaves have a sweet aroma, making them one of the most appealing of all deciduous American trees.

Meanwhile I was designing a stone terrace on the southern side of the house from where one could enjoy the views down the slope of the lawn to the native trees beyond. This terrace would be an outdoor room — the part of the garden most lived in by my clients — and would be another formal element.

I spent several days searching for a local stone that could be sawn into random rectangles for the terrace. Since such a thing proved impossible to find, we finally opted for New York bluestone, which occurs as either a bluey-green or a grey stone. We chose the grey version which creates much the same crisp effect when sawn as English Yorkstone.

Demanding perfection as always, my clients decided that instead of leaving it to the stonemason's discretion, I should specify in a plan the proportions of each individual stone slab that made up the fifty metres of terrace. The mason would then cut the stones on site according to the plan. It was an immense task, and one that took several days to accomplish, even with the aid of a full-time draftsman.

In designing good paving, the secret is to make it as simple as possible. It is unfortunate if paving draws undue attention to itself. In this instance, the effect created was understated and harmonious. When looking down the length of the terrace, at right angles to the house, there were interesting perspectives. To the west, it ended in a group of mature sugar maples. To the east, it ran across a lawn and into a tiny orchard of three apple trees. To the south, it looked out across the lawn and into mature trees.

It was important to keep the slopes of the garden here relatively clear of trees so that we could 'borrow' the view of trees from the vast, otherwise empty, hectares of neighbouring Cranbrook School. Between this slope, however, and the small convex slope on a different plane, facing away from the house to the east, the natural terrain created a descending ridge. Here I suggested that we plant a forest of indigenous canoe birches, *Betula papyrifera*, to demarcate one part of the garden from the other. The following spring we planted thirty-one large specimens of these attractive trees, with their flaking paper-white bark and interesting autumn colour.

Of all the small woods in the garden, this one is probably the simplest and most dramatic. At night it is lit with a gentle wash from halogen lights so that it can be seen from a table at which the family often dines.

The formality of the paved terrace suggested herbaceous borders, which would ease the transition to the informal woodland area of the garden beyond. So consumed did we become with the herbaceous borders that for several years we employed a brilliant young Belgian horticulturalist, Bernard Dogimont, a former student of the Kalmthout Arboretum, to ensure that the beds were looking their best at all times of the year.

The borders here were partly shaded, and so as not to compete with the broader garden views beyond, my clients decided that all the flowers should be shell-pink. Anything resembling red was instantly removed. In the shade, hostas, thalictrum, astilbes and tiarella thrived, creating a soft and pleasing effect. In the sunny parts of the beds herbaceous paeonies, penstemon, *Dicentra spectabilis*, *Centranthus ruber*, platycodon and *Astrantia major* were found to be reliable allies. Then, in the autumn, Japanese anemones, *Sedum* 'Autumn Joy' and the pendulous flowers of *Hydrangea paniculata* 'Grandiflora', took over.

The front of the house was effectively a gravelled courtyard, and here herbaceous borders were created, this time in a broad spectrum of blue, mauve and white flowers. Plants such as hostas, *Bergenia cordifolia*, *Lysimachia clethroides* and rodgersia were useful for their architectural foliage. In spring and early summer, lots of sky-blue flowers were provided by anchusa, brunnera, pulmonaria, *Centaurea montana* and tradescantia. At the height of the season, salvia, veronica and delphinium were the happiest hunting ground for the sky-blue and light-mauve-coloured flowers that were needed. We were also dependent upon plants like scabiosa, nepeta, iris, echinops, *Catananche caerulea* and aconites to maintain the sense of excitement. Blue-flowering clematis and morning glories continued the theme of the garden beds onto the walls of the house. These wide blue borders did much to create a soft and welcoming effect for anyone arriving at the house through the entrance courtyard.

The Bloomfield Hills garden represents how well formal and informal elements of garden design can be combined to the best advantage of a site. Here, lines of formality cut through seas of informality, making the garden more liveable for people whilst interfering as little as possible with the inherent integrity of the site. This garden could not have been achieved without the patience and commitment of my clients, who were sympathetic with my basic philosophy. Whenever all three of us happened to be in Detroit at the same time we would regularly spend evenings together – sometimes late into the night – discussing all aspects of the garden's design and maintenance.

If this garden is a success it is because we worked as a team, only proceeding with a project once we all concurred. I attempt to visit Michigan at least once a year to keep an eye on how it is developing, as it is one of my favourite gardens.

OPPOSITE *The creation of mood is everything in the design of a garden. This scene owes its mood not so much to the flowers as to the modulation of light and shade by the surrounding deciduous trees.*

a

VEGETABLE

garden

D uring a regular visit to the Bloomfield Hills garden, my clients asked me to design a vegetable garden. They had a chef and wished to grow their own fresh vegetables and herbs. Furthermore, they wanted the vegetable garden to be as close to the kitchen door as possible, which meant siting it in the most unattractive part of the garden: a no-man's-land housing the airconditioning unit and a concrete dog run, to which we had previously not given much thought.

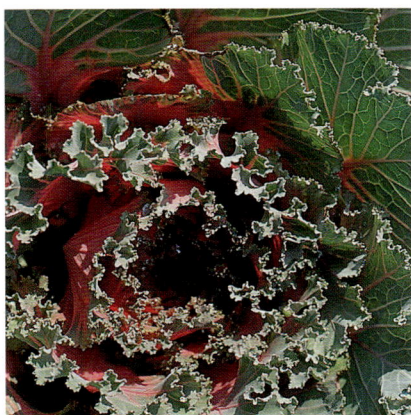

Here grew a badly positioned apple tree and a few haphazard and meaningless garden beds, all the legacy of previous owners.

Given such unimpressive raw material, I was not enthusiastic about the idea and hoped it might be forgotten. I could not see how a vegetable garden might fit into the rest of the garden. I sat down at my drawing board and knocked out a plan, which left me totally cold. The more I studied the proposed site the more I was confounded by its limitations.

The roughly triangular shape of the area that I had to work within seemed ill-suited to a working vegetable garden. On its far side lay the boundary of the garden, beyond which stood a group of pines. On its southern side, the relatively level ground fell away to a convex-shaped wilderness below, the top of this slope thus creating the second side of the triangle. The third side of the triangle was determined by the need to keep the geometry simple and the vegetable garden at a reasonable distance from the house. This last consideration was important. I needed some space in which to screen the vegetable garden within hedges and trees – thus partially disassociating it from the house – whilst keeping it within a practical distance from the kitchen.

The second time I looked at the problem, however, the entire jigsaw puzzle fell into place with tantalising speed. By a stroke of good fortune, the apex of the triangle – where the boundary of the garden met the point where the level ground started to fall away – was in line with the centre of the bluestone terrace I had designed the previous year. This would become the principal axial line.

Now that my emerging design had a main axis, it was a question of deciding what kind of events would occur along its length. The ill-sited apple tree obviously would have to be moved, but – and here was the second piece of good fortune – if it were added to the three apple trees planted closer to the house, a *walk* of four apple trees could be created along the axial line. Rarely had solving a design problem given me so much pleasure. I then realised that if I planted a tall yew hedge on the northern side of the Apple Walk, it would emphasise the importance of the apple trees and help lead the eye down to the vegetable garden. It would also have the inestimable advantage of hiding the large airconditioning unit. In order not to make the Apple Walk too claustrophobic, I decided to add low yew hedges on its opposite, or southern, side.

It has been said that good garden design depends upon changes of level as much as any other factor. Such facile dicta don't always bear too much scrutiny, but on balance there is much to be said in favour of this one. Changes of level in gardens can add an indefinable element of mystery, particularly when making the transition from one part of the garden to the next.

[62]

Fortunately I was able to end the Apple Walk in a semicircular flight of steps, which would lead down to the vegetable garden. Here the eye would be engaged by a circular pond, its surface as level to the ground as possible so as to best reflect the sky. To ensure that it was in scale with the rest of the vegetable garden, the pool was placed close to the bottom of the semicircular steps: it simply didn't work in the centre of the space.

The focal point of the pond – indeed of the entire vista from the terrace and house – would be a water jet, several metres high, illuminated at night by underwater lights. This jet could be regulated according to mood so that when the garden was not *en fête* it could be turned down to become a mere welling on the surface of the pool, creating gentle concentric ripples, or else be turned off altogether.

In those days I was living in Spain and had come under the spell of the Moorish gardens of the Alhambra and the Generalife in Granada. It occurred to me that here was an opportunity to design this vegetable

PREVIOUS PAGES *The lower vegetable garden was designed to be seen from above, between the foliage of the apple trees which were transplanted onto the intervening bank.* RIGHT *The design of this garden is more apparent from the air. From the tree-shaded terrace at the back of the house, one turns left and passes through the hedged Apple Walk to reach the upper vegetable garden with its circular pond. From here the lower vegetable garden can only be discovered upon reaching the narrow rectangular platform that overlooks it.*

garden as a hybrid between a formal parterre in the French style and a Moorish patio. I was also interested in Thomas Jefferson's garden at Monticello, which combined French formality with a distinctly American character. I, too, wanted the formal vegetable garden to be distinctly American in tone, even though the initial inspiration for it came from Europe.

I was also subtly influenced by certain contemporary American artists like Sol Lewitt and the interesting geometry of some of their work. In arranging the garden beds and paths around the circular pond, I ended up with a composition which – when viewed logically as a whole – was the remains of a square-shaped parterre that had been tilted on its side and then had almost half its area cut off. Interestingly, this sliced-off portion of a larger, symmetrical parterre was in itself symmetrical. It was, effectively, *punning* in geometry, and it worked.

My clients were immediately enthusiastic about the design and we started construction in late 1985. Along the boundary on the far side of the garden I designed a two-metre-high brick wall. We also started to look for a ready-grown yew hedge that would instantly look as if it had always bordered the Apple Walk. After

much searching we were told of a forty-year-old hedge on an estate close to Montauk, Long Island, which we eventually agreed to buy. The box plants needed to hedge each of the garden beds were also difficult to find, simply because we needed so many. Once again we wished to create an instant effect, and in the end we found mature plants in Springfield, Illinois.

It was a fascinating job deciding which vegetables would look good together in the same bed. My clients were particularly concerned that this composition be both practical and aesthetically pleasing. 'But if we were to choose between those two requirements,' they concurred, 'it would be that the garden be aesthetically pleasing.' The rate of growth of each vegetable and its time of harvesting had to be taken into account. It was all

ABOVE and OPPOSITE *Since frosts can be expected until mid- to late May, the beds in the upper vegetable garden are planted with tulip bulbs in the autumn so as to give a spectacular flash of colour in early May. The frost-tender vegetable plants and herbs can be bedded out later in the month. The focal point of this garden is a circular pond with a jet of water.*

[64]

very well, for example, to plant tomatoes and cabbages in the same bed, but from June to September the tomatoes would shade the cabbages out of existence. Lettuces, on the other hand, grow very quickly and could be picked before the tomato plants became too large.

For the most part, Detroit is a sprawling city of immense, rather impersonal spaces. Like many modern American cities, the inhuman quality of its scale can leave you feeling vaguely uneasy and alienated. What I most enjoy about this parterre garden is that on returning to it from driving on the freeways it restores my confidence in the human stature and acts as an antidote to the feeling of urban infinity. With the calm splash of its jet of water, its sense of order and abundance, it is a place in which one can relax and meditate.

On the vegetable garden's completion, I jokingly suggested to my clients that since this garden had been so much fun to make, they should commission me to create another one, further down the slope in the convex-shaped wilderness. They simply laughed at such an idea. A few months later, however, I was bidden to Detroit for a special meeting. Over dinner, and not without some teasing and endearing theatricality, my clients announced that they wanted to go ahead and build a second parterre vegetable garden. There would now be an upper vegetable garden and a lower vegetable garden. I started work on the design the following morning.

I already knew how I wanted the garden to actually work. From the terrace in front of the house one's eye would be drawn down the Apple Walk, towards the first vegetable garden, where it would be caught by the jet of water. Since the change in level prevented the water of the pond from immediately being seen, this created an air of mystery. Wondering where the jet was coming from would involuntarily draw one's feet after one's eye to answer the riddle.

Once this issue had been solved, another mystery presented itself. The upper vegetable garden is enclosed on all sides but the southern. Here the parterre ends in a void, created by the steeply falling bank. Once again, one's feet are drawn after the eye to discover what happens in the apparently empty space. Here the second parterre would be created which, unlike the first, could be viewed from above, almost as if from a bird's-eye view.

The construction of the lower parterre was going to be more complicated than the upper one simply because the bank needed to be attacked by bulldozers in order to create a level area of ground for the garden. This meant that the bank linking the two gardens would be steep. To create drama, I designed a double flight of steps, each with two landings on the way down. Because I intended the inspiration of this

PREVIOUS PAGES *It was important that the double flight of steps leading into the lower vegetable garden be sculptural, suggesting two cascades of water in suspended animation.* ABOVE *Bronze-foliaged fennel contrasts well with a blue-foliaged brassica, creating a turbulent sea of foliage in which the urn acts as a stable focal point.* OPPOSITE *Vegetables are amongst the most decorative of all plants.*

complex of vegetable gardens to continue owing as much to American civilisation as to European, the steps were designed with the ancient temples of the Toltecs, Aztecs and Mayas in mind. Of particular inspiration was the Sun Temple of Teotihuacán, and the steps facing the huge plaza at Monte Albán, both of which are in present-day Mexico. Of greatest importance in my mind was that the steps be sculptural, suggesting two cascades of water in suspended animation.

The impact of all this masonry would need softening, and the idea of creating a copse between the two vegetable gardens was enormously appealing. A dozen small trees were needed which, since they formed part of a formal layout, did not necessarily have to be Michigan natives. As a result, a dozen fully mature apple trees found in an Ohio orchard were delivered in a convoy of six semitrailers the following spring and planted on the grassy bank. This part of Michigan is famous for apple trees, and the copse ties in happily with the Apple Walk above.

Since it was decided that all the very large vegetables – such as maize, pumpkins and potatoes – would be grown in the lower vegetable garden, it was important that the design of the beds themselves be interesting. We decided upon four classically simple but different patterns. Once again each bed would be hedged with box plants, and the garden itself would be enclosed on three sides by a yew hedge. Since one of the neighbouring houses overlooked the garden, we decided to screen it with pleached trees. Hornbeams of any size were impossible to find in the United States, and pleached beech trees were going to be a little too coarsely textured and heavy. In the end we found some large field maples, *Acer campestre*, and over the years they have proved excellent as a result of both their hardiness and their ability to tolerate pruning.

My clients were particularly concerned that the vegetable garden be screened from the road which ran along its southern perimeter. To achieve this, ten white pine trees, *Pinus strobus*, were planted very closely together on the road's edge. These trees are remarkably tolerant and don't mind being transplanted as large specimens. And being native, they also grow comparatively quickly. But I wished to avoid a wall of pine trees as the immediate backdrop to the vegetable garden. Another tree would be needed in the space purposely left between the end of the vegetable garden and the group of pines.

I was looking for something very simple yet dramatic, and disliking the fussy effect that can be created by a jumble of different trees, I felt that this could best be achieved by planting many of the same type of tree. *Say it once and say it strongly* is excellent counsel. It was important that such a tree also be sympathetic with the fruiting apple trees on the bank. Much thought and agonising went into this issue. Finishing a garden is usually the hardest part of all: you have struggled to create something special and are terrified by the spectre of ruining it all with a last-minute error.

It was at Princeton Nurseries in New Jersey that I finally came across a field of excellent crab-apple trees, *Malus × zumi*, and in the end we ordered eighteen. These crab-apple trees are smothered in pure white flowers in spring and create a striking effect, particularly as their flowering coincides with that of the apple trees on the bank. And even though photographs of the flowering apple and crab apples make them look identical in colour, they are in reality quite different. The fruiting apple trees have distinctly cream-coloured flowers, attractively flecked with subtle streaks of pink.

The principal purpose of the lower vegetable garden, apart from its practical function of producing vegetables for the kitchen, is to create a view for the garden above. Unlike in the upper vegetable garden, which is primarily decorative, I am never tempted to loiter within its confines, either to relax or to meditate. This is very much a working garden.

a
ROSE
garden

N umber 8, The Esplanade, is one of the oldest houses in Peppermint Grove, in Perth. It has the air of an Australian country homestead, and overlooks a broad reach of the Swan River. The light in Perth shines with the brilliance of a revelation, and in the early mornings, before the wind gets up, the surface of the water has a remarkable opalescent quality.

Apart from its striking views onto the Swan River — which at this point more closely resembles a vast lake — the other notable feature of this town garden is its generous size. Between the house and The Esplanade the terrain slopes away gently towards the road, beyond which it falls abruptly towards the river through indigenous bushland.

What brings the garden to life are the birds. The tall umbrella, or stone, pines are populated with magpies; a family of kookaburras and flocks of 'twenty-eight' parrots regularly fly in to visit. These birds, with their bright-green bodies and yellow necks, are named twenty-eights because as they chatter away in the trees, it sounds as if they are saying 'twenty-eight . . . twenty-eight . . .'. I was initially asked to visit the garden for a couple of hours to suggest ideas for this front garden by David and Marie Louise Wordsworth and their daughter Sara.

My first thought was that the entire garden was wasted as a result of the black bitumen drive that cut through it. The circular drive entered from a side street, passed directly in front of the house and made its way through the garden to The Esplanade in the far corner. What's more, the entire front garden was in full view of the street. This was unfortunate. The area was clearly large enough to create an interesting living space close to the house: something with a real sense of privacy that might be enjoyed.

As a garden designer I sometimes find consultations like this quite difficult. A number of questions inevitably flash through my mind. How committed are the clients to changing the garden? Do they want a few ideas to make quick fixes or do they want to make fundamental changes? In many cases I don't think the clients themselves know the answers to such questions until they have sounded out the possibilities.

There was just such an air of uncertainty during the first hour of our discussions about the garden. Then I sat down to lunch with three generations of Wordsworths — each family member giving ideas as to how the garden might be developed. We ate on the verandah that extends along much of the front of the house, sitting behind a veil of climbing roses, bougainvillea and wisteria. It was a delightful place to be, in cool and scented shade, and looking towards the river bathed in bright sunlight.

Nonetheless, I couldn't help feeling that life on the verandah would be much more pleasant if the nearby drive could be transformed into foliage, if the noise of traffic could be muffled by the sound of falling water, and if the air could be made a little cooler. This, however, would mean sacrificing the convenience of being able to drive right up to the front door of the house. In the end it didn't take much persuasion: the Wordsworths had long dreamt of having a rose garden, and quickly agreed to the sacrifice. Once this decision was made, I was commissioned to design a large formal rose garden which would run across the entire façade of the house, just below the verandah.

The key to this garden would be to treat it relatively informally so that it didn't conflict with its surroundings. The house had been built in the late nineteenth century, in what is called Early Federation style, a fashion that had its origins in the emerging garden suburbs of Victorian London. Too much formality might have looked pretentious and imposed. As it happens, box plants do not grow happily in Perth, and so the temptation of bordering the rose beds with neatly clipped hedges — and thus turning up the volume of formality — was not presented to us. Even so, the question of formality worried me well beyond my first visit to Perth.

It was only months later, in Paris, in one of the world's best-known formal rose gardens, that an answer suddenly occurred to me. The southern end of the rose garden at Bagatelle is enclosed by tall wooden posts from which ropes are strung to create generous swags that support a profusion of climbing roses. Although symmetrical, the upright posts and crossbeams have a delightfully informal air. I thought that something similar to this would solve the problem of formality in the rose garden in Perth.

The basic ground plan of the rose garden had been designed during my first visit. There would still be a drive, but henceforth it would cut across the front lawn on the far side of the rose garden. The verandah and front door of the house could now be approached only on foot, by way of the rose garden. The new garden would occupy almost precisely the same space as the old tarmac drive.

PREVIOUS PAGES *The large garden table sitting in the shade of a pine tree can only just be seen through the densely planted beds of shrub roses.* BELOW *Inspired by the rose garden at Bagatelle in Paris, roses climb the posts and are then trained into swags along the ropes hanging from post to post.*

Indeed, the main part of the rose garden would lie directly in front of the steps that led to the front door of the house. At its southern end, a change of level would take one down half a metre to a separate, smaller garden. The lower level of the rose garden would be a square enclosure which — unlike the larger upper level — would be surrounded on two sides by a two-metre-high limestone wall. This would create the effect of a private and comfortably proportioned outdoor room.

At the centre of this enclosure, I designed a raised fish pond, the scale of which was purposely large in comparison with its surroundings to give it something of the feeling of the tank pool at Hidcote. The Wordsworths wanted a large Victorian wrought-iron fountain to be placed at the centre of the pond, and that meant making the pond larger still, otherwise the fountain would have looked overly mannered. Although my clients were initially concerned about having such a large pond, in the end they embraced the idea.

Apart from following the existing contours of the garden, the main reason for this smaller, square enclosure was to give a view to that part of the verandah on which the Wordsworths often had lunch. It was important that the sight and sound of the pond and fountain be enjoyed as much from the southern end of the verandah as from the garden below. The fact that the pond was raised above ground level, and that the fountain was much higher again, helped create a pleasant proximity between the water and those people sitting on the verandah.

Whilst this lower garden, with the fountain at its centre, was very much a place in which to sit and relax, the upper rectangular garden was designed primarily as a place in which to stroll. It was important that the plants be allowed to fall over the paths and blur the strict lines of the garden's formality. Nevertheless, the upper garden was laid out as a symmetrical parterre centred on the verandah's front steps. As the plants grew larger, this symmetry would serve a practical purpose, enabling a large number of roses to be grown in a relatively small

ABOVE *The source of the stones for this one-metre-high retaining wall was an old demolished rockery in the garden. The wall was carefully designed to take full advantage of the potential of each individual stone.* OPPOSITE *In a climate such as Perth's, where easterly winds in summer blow in from the desert, gardens designed as oases are most appealing. The focal point of this entire rose garden is the pond and its fountain, which present the spectacle — and sound — of abundant water.*

TOP *The limestone paths and steps were laid in such a way that groundcover plants could grow in the interstices and claim much of the walking space as their own.* ABOVE *In summer the rose garden is sprayed with water several times a day. Not only is this visually appealing, but it also brings to the garden a marvellous sensual quality.*

space, without imposing a style that might be too stark or contradictory in relation to the house. The garden's outer edge would be defined by a wall of roses climbing up the wooden posts and along the swags. These posts and ropes, however, looked very naked until the climbing roses began to grow, and it was little wonder that a wit at the Weld Club in Perth nicknamed it 'Marie Louise's OK Corral'.

To lend a sense of arrival, a wooden pergola was placed over the short flight of steps leading from the drive to the parterre, on the way to the house. The line running through this pergola, from the front door of the house onto the Swan River, created the main axis of the garden.

Whereas this axial line was essentially concerned with getting people to the front door as quickly and as simply as possible, I considered the upper garden's cross-axis to be more important aesthetically. To the right, on the garden's southern side, one's eye would be drawn by the sight of water bubbling up into the air and catching the light, from the fountain in the lower garden. To the left, on the northern side, stood a large umbrella pine, *Pinus pinea*. This large tree on the garden's perimeter provided a strong focal point.

Since roses would not grow beneath the pine tree, this end of the garden was paved, making it one step higher than the parterre. A large table was also placed here, creating an alternative place to have lunch. I have since noticed with pleasure that the Wordsworths eat here often. Apart from this spot, there is nowhere else to sit in the parterre garden, and it remains a garden for walking through.

In contrast, two seats were placed in the lower rose garden: one at the end of the main axis, in line with the fountain; and the other beneath a bower of climbing roses in pleasant shade, so that one could sit and see without being seen. To give the lower garden dappled shade during the hotter months of the year, I recommended planting three flowering peach trees. I particularly like the colour of the foliage of these trees – a bluey-green that gives a sense of coolness in such a hot climate. The peach trees' long, slender leaves are an added attraction, and since peaches belong to the rose family, they have the virtue of associating well with roses.

The hills behind Perth are known to be one of the best places in the world in which to grow roses. They grow here with that slightly unreal perfection for which the hothouse roses at the Chelsea Flower Show are famous. The only difference is that in Perth they grow out-of-doors. And in massed plantings, they present an astonishing spectacle.

We went to Bob Melville's nursery in the hills to select the best roses for the Wordsworth's garden. Conditions in the suburbs of Perth are not as ideal for many types of rose as those in the hills, and so we discussed the possibilities carefully. We knew that David Austin hybrids would thrive, and Marie Louise and Sara chose as many as possible. As climbing roses for the swags and the posts in between, 'Black Boy', with deep red flowers and 'Kathleen Harrop', one of the thornless roses with attractive pink flowers, were chosen. But they have also proved popular with the twenty-eights, and the parrots often swoop in and eat the young rose shoots before they have a chance to produce flowers.

I had mentioned to the Wordsworths that once construction of the rose garden was completed, the remainder of the front garden would be thrown into sharp contrast and might begin to look odd in comparison. Indeed from the start, a ragbag of plants with an indecisive air growing along the garden's boundaries threatened to detract from the integrity of the rest of the garden. As a result, I suggested we plant an informal hedge which would extend from the rose garden around the entire front garden and which, ultimately, would give both house and garden privacy from the street and footpath. Once again my clients were quick to understand the issues involved. They suggested planting camellias.

Initially, this idea concerned me. Perth has long summers during which easterly winds blow in from the desert as if from a blast furnace. Most camellias prefer cool and shady parts of the garden. I had no previous experience of growing camellias in Perth, and so I asked the Wordsworths if they knew of an expert who might advise us. As luck had it, they knew Jean Evans of the Australian Camellia Research Society, who agreed to come out and inspect the site. Jean pronounced it suitable for a limited number of camellia hybrids including 'Kramer's Supreme', 'Tomorrow', 'Georgia Rouse' and 'Great Eastern'. These, she assured us, could thrive under the adverse conditions.

Perth is still a small enough city for people to take a friendly interest in the goings-on of those around them. All sorts of people saw us planting the camellia hedge and volunteered the information that it would die the following summer. Fortunately, Jean Evans knew what she was talking about and they were proved wrong. Indeed, all the camellias survived the summer heat. The pundits, however, were unconvinced. Bets were placed at the Weld Club as to how long it would be before they died. The camellias, meanwhile, lived on – though they certainly took their time becoming established. It was almost as if they were malingering on purpose, tantalising the neighbourhood with the spectre that they might, at any moment, comply with the general prophecy. It took three summers to demonstrate beyond reasonable doubt their ability not only to survive but to thrive.

Perhaps the greatest pleasure this garden gives me is that each time I visit Perth the Wordsworths say how much it has improved each day of their lives. And no garden designer can fail to be moved by that.

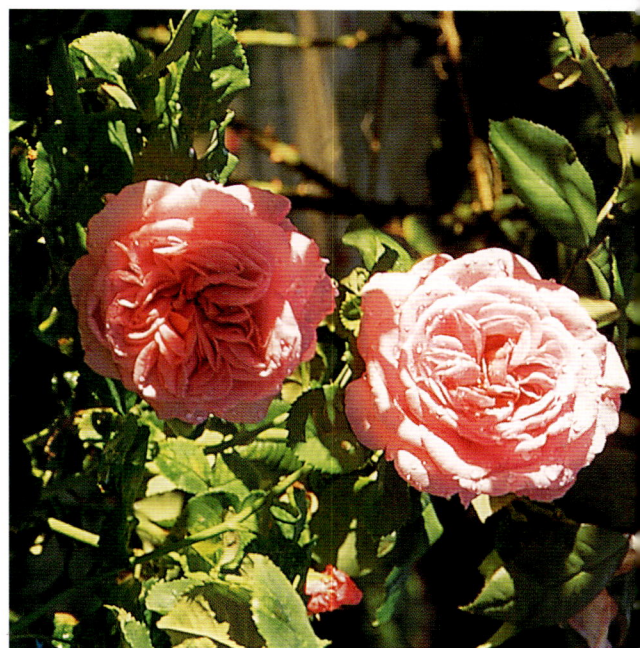

TOP *It was decided that deep red and pink roses would be used in the garden to the exclusion of all others. The pink rose is 'Else Poulsen' and the red rose is 'Lilli Marlene'.* ABOVE *'Mary Rose'.*

a MEDITERRANEAN *garden*

In 1983 I was invited to be the landscape designer for a Spanish development company in Palma de Mallorca. The company had bought a huge tract of land that extended upwards from the sea at Illetas for several kilometres to the top of a mountain range. The urbanisation, as it was called, was planned as a new suburb for the city of Palma de Mallorca. And this is what it has become.

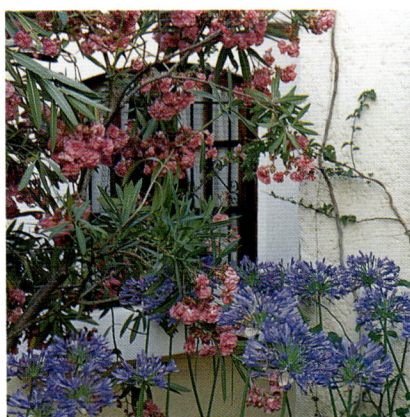

I signed a contract with the company to work for them for several years and so my immediate concern was to find somewhere to live near Palma. The idea of an apartment in the city was not appealing. Pat Samuel, the president of the company and my boss, organised for me to be shown a ruined shepherd's house, high up a mountain in what was called the Parque del Rey.

This is the mountain that lies behind both the urbanisation and the site of the future golf course, rising to a height of several thousand metres above sea level. Its lower slopes had been cleared many centuries ago and carved into olive terraces of dry limestone walls. Here and there amongst the olive trees, a carob tree, *Ceratonia siliqua*, would cast its deep shade. The peasants who had once tended these olive trees had long gone, and native pine trees had started to seed themselves once more. The company planned to one day sell off the land as estates of approximately eight hectares each. However, because of the steepness of parts of the mountain, much of it would be left untouched as natural wilderness.

The steep sides of the mountain were a spectacular sight as we wound along the rough dirt track, making our way towards the ridge on which the ruined cottage stood. The first sight of my future house, barely discernible through the undergrowth, was of a wall of dressed limestone boulders with a gaping hole where there had once been a window.

No one knew how long the cottage had been there, although it was said to date from at least the fourteenth century, if not from Roman times. Graffiti on its walls testified to the fact that it hadn't been lived in since World War Two, and it had long ago lost its roof and almost one entire wall. There were only three rooms, each of about sixteen square metres, and these were filled with large self-sown pine saplings and shrubs. But its walls, including the internal ones, were one metre thick and the ceilings – once they were rebuilt – would be high, making the house cool in summer and warm in winter.

What attracted me to this small cottage on first sight was its remoteness. On three sides it was surrounded by folds in the mountain and a forest of indigenous Aleppo pines, *Pinus halepensis*. On its fourth and southern side it had a commanding view, through terraces of olive and carob trees, over the entire Bay of Palma. The seaside suburbs of Palma were about two kilometres away, below us. But here on the mountain, there was wilderness with no neighbours.

I entered into an agreement with the company to live in the cottage and immediately began working to make it habitable. So captivated was I by the magic of the place that I decided to interfere with the existing landscape as little as possible. The dry hillside, once cultivated by peasant farmers, was quickly returning to *maquis*: low-growing scrub that colonises dry, uncultivated regions all over the Mediterranean. Growing wild and covering the ground around the cottage were rosemary, rock roses, lavender and a low broom with silver foliage. The smell of their leaves and that of the resinous pines mixed in the hot summer air to create an unforgettably rich, Mediterranean scent.

The intention was to restore the stone walls of the olive terraces, and to care for the olive and carob trees growing there. I also wished to allow the indigenous perennials to take over at ground level and to cut paths through them. I saw myself not as a cultivator but as an editor of the natural environment surrounding the house. For example, there were too many shrubs of mastic, or *Pistacia lentiscus*, growing close to the house and on the surrounding terraces, and they impeded access. Many of these I removed, thus enabling the rosemary, lavender and rock roses to take their place.

I had no desire to have lawns and garden beds of bright flowers. I wanted my garden to be a tamed Mediterranean wilderness, following the natural rhythms of the seasons. During the summer months it rarely rained, and I remember at least two years when no rain fell for a stretch of more than twelve weeks. During these months, when the winds blew from Africa, you could sense the proximity of the Sahara Desert as you involuntarily inhaled its fine airborne dust. The perennials and low shrubs became very dry and stressed in this season, but this was part of their annual cycle. It is the dryness and heat that causes their foliage to smell so sweetly and haunt the air.

PREVIOUS PAGES *The bold architectural foliage of* Yucca elephantipes *and the soft-pink flowers of oleander create interesting contrasts against the powder-pink façade of the Anchorage apartments.* RIGHT *I restored the cottage in the background, which overlooks the Bay of Palma, and lived there whilst working in Spain. In the foreground is the long stone* cisterna *from which my household water came.*

For outdoor living I needed a large shaded terrace from where to enjoy the view, and so a pergola along the entire front of the house was constructed. Here were laid terra cotta tiles, made by a farmer with a simple kiln in a remote valley. After the tiles had been baked, their rough underside appealed more than their smooth side, and so I decided to have them laid upside down instead.

Although I grew star jasmine to provide shade for the terrace, this took time establishing itself. Meanwhile I laid panels of slatted bamboo across the top of the pergola. This terrace became an outdoor sitting room and dining room, which could be used at night from May until October. Many memorable dinner parties were held here in these heroically simple surroundings.

My first job for the development company was the landscaping of a new housing development called the Garden Villas, about a kilometre further down the mountain from my house. The Garden Villas were two distinct clusters of town houses arranged around separate courtyards and designed by a local architect, Pedro Otzoup. The two clusters were separated by a wide lawn at the end of which was a swimming pool. From an architectural point of view it was a clever use of the site since, apart from the extensive communal gardens, each town house had its own private garden. Such an arrangement provided interesting possibilities for garden design.

Whereas on the mountain, around my stone house, I was free to garden as I pleased, here I was under a major constraint. This was a commercial venture and my job was to provide instant gardens to help boost sales. The Garden Villas were constructed in suburban surroundings, and each of the private gardens, the two courtyards and the large central lawn were inward-looking, being surrounded by houses on all sides.

A subtropical garden that enhanced a sense of privacy – making its enclosed nature a virtue – would be the best way to create an instant impact. The first garden for the pilot house would pretend it was an oasis with a bountiful supply of water. Like the harbour garden I had made in Vaucluse in Sydney five years previously, it would have a disciplined planting scheme. Unlike that garden, it would be protected by walls, and the foliage would provide its sole focus.

I immediately scoured the local nurseries in a Land Rover looking for suitable plants. In those days the local nurseries mainly sold small plants and anything fully grown had to come from the Spanish mainland, but I was able to find several large specimens of bamboo and hibiscus. I also used banana trees and canna lilies, choosing the latter with deep-green foliage and shocking pink flowers.

Since the purchasers we were aiming to attract were British, German and Swiss it was important to include a lawn in the design. As in bushland settings in Australia, I prefer generally to avoid lawns in Mediterranean countries since they tend to look false next to indigenous plants. In this case, however, my scruples were assuaged by the fact that the lawn was within an enclosed garden and had no pretensions of forming part of the wider natural landscape.

The subtropical oasis garden for the pilot house was judged a success by John Kay, the company's director of marketing, and so I decided to extend this theme into one of the large communal courtyards. The second courtyard was to have its own very different character. Here I used plants that are tolerant of the dry Mediterranean climate, although on the central lawn between the two groups of houses, subtropical palms would again be used. In all of these enclosures, water would be the clearly discernible focal point: in each of the two courtyards, there would be a raised circular pond with a central jet of water; on the central lawn, there would be the swimming pool.

Although each of the garden beds in the courtyards were designed to be rectilinear – some of them at ground level and others raised – the effect of the gardens was informal rather than formal. The reason for raising some of the beds was not only to give a reasonable depth of soil where there was otherwise rocky ground, but also to give the new plants precocious height, thereby creating an instant effect. The raised beds also served to hide various parts of the garden, lending an air of mystery. Normally I consider boring those gardens that can be seen in their entirety from one vantage point.

The architectural elements of the two gardens – their walls, paths, steps, water features and lawns – needed to be carefully handled. The placing of these structural elements sets a pattern in the same, if less obvious, way as it does in a formal garden, thus establishing and reinforcing the garden's basic rhythms. Even in an informal garden, a conscious rhythm must be adopted and observed in order to create a disciplined design, where otherwise there will be only chaos.

Thus, despite their informality, each of the Garden Villas' gardens offered clear focal points along distinct axial lines. In some instances, the

PREVIOUS PAGES *During the summer months, this arch of bougainvillea in the Mediterranean courtyard in the Garden Villas provides a dramatic splash of colour when seen against the sober scheme of blue-flowering agapanthus, an Italian cypress and a pepper tree,* Schinus molle. BELOW *The first concern in designing the gardens of the Anchorage was to save the indigenous forest of Aleppo pines,* Pinus halepensis, *so as to preserve the spirit of the place. Wherever possible the design of the steps and retaining walls was done in the local idiom.*

focal point was one of the circular ponds. In others, it was an interesting tree or the swimming pool. The simpler the axial line, the more effective it is. Capability Brown was the great master of simplicity, and he often used a sequence of enfolding promontories of trees between which there was an informal vista leading the eye up to a folly or perhaps a clump of trees of different character.

These simple mechanics work no matter what the scale. The sense of interlocking promontories of foliage along a vista — together with, perhaps, a change of level via a flight of steps — and an interesting plant acting as an exclamation mark is all that it takes to create a sense of relaxed order. In settings such as these courtyards, all that is needed is a lightly imposed discipline. Too much discipline in such surroundings creates the wrong mood.

The subtropical courtyard initially grew faster and better than the Mediterranean courtyard. Automatic watering systems were installed in both, and the Mediterranean garden suffered from overwatering.

After the courtyard gardens were completed, a pundit in the company said that they were too simple and needed spicing up. He suggested adding some white plaster *pretending-to-be-marble* statues as well as that most unattractive of all Spanish horticultural clichés, the half-buried terra cotta pot. I begged to differ and felt that this was the end of the matter.

Several months later, returning from a long working trip to the United States and Australia, I discovered terra cotta pots submerged in the centre of some of the garden beds, along with some sparkling new white plaster statues of sentimentally posed huntresses, their arms wrapped amorously around the necks of lions. Water dribbled from the lions' mouths.

It was an easy matter to unearth and smash the pots and throw away the rubble. But the statues, by contrast, had been cemented in place. My boss, Pat Samuel, saw the humorous side of this and laughed when told the tale. But the firmly anchored white plaster statues, and their expensive submersible pumps which created the dribble, remained to reproach my design.

It was on the Anchorage, a complex of apartments to be built on a small rocky cove on the edge of the Mediterranean, that the company placed the most emphasis. The site was remarkable, not only for its beauty but also because of its apparent remoteness from the surrounding suburbs. So perfect was this sense of isolation that the beach had long been Palma's only nudist beach and this situation continued until, protesting loudly, the naked were driven away by the arrival of bulldozers and excavators.

A single, long articulated building – which would be the first phase of the Anchorage development – would wrap around the cove, giving most of the apartments a view directly onto the Bay of Palma. On a large terrace facing the sea, situated where the eastern and western arms of the building converged to create a large 'U', would be the swimming pool. This swimming-pool courtyard would serve as the site of the Anchorage Club, which it was planned would have one of the best restaurants and bars on the island.

François Spoerry, who was responsible for Port Grimaud near St Tropez in the south of France, was chosen as the architect. And Prince Alfonso von Hohenlohe, founder and director of the well-known Marbella Club in southern Spain, would set up and run the Anchorage Club. This made a fascinating team with which to work because these two men possibly knew more about creating developments of the highest quality in the western Mediterranean than anyone else.

It was instructive to watch von Hohenlohe in action on his home ground at the Marbella Club: no single detail, from the napkins on the restaurant tables to the type of soil used in the terra cotta pots, escaped him. He understood, above all else, the unfrivolous art of creating magic, which resulted in the escapist mood of the Marbella Club and its gardens. At night the character of his gardens in Marbella changed completely with the mysterious interplay of light and dark, and the tenebrous shadows. And to achieve this he used both electricity and candlelight with a subtle mastery.

The pine forest in which the Anchorage was to be built was identical to the one in which I lived on the mountain behind. I wanted to preserve as much of it as possible, right down to the edge of the sea. Here stunted pines grew on the rocks and overhung the water as in classical Chinese landscape paintings. On a coastline where much of the indigenous character had been erased, I was determined not to contribute to further unnecessary destruction. And after my experience at the Garden Villas, I knew the potential savagery of Spanish builders with regard to native trees, since many pine trees there had been pointlessly destroyed.

As a result, I ensured that the trees I wished to preserve at the Anchorage were boxed in with metal shuttering. To emphasise the point further, I organised for a penalty clause to be placed in the building contract so that if any trees were accidentally or wilfully killed, the builders would be fined. To my pleasant surprise this actually worked. After eighteen months of building, we were left with all but one of the native trees intact.

Whilst the seashore itself was to be left unaltered, every apartment on the ground floor would have its own private garden facing the sea. These would each have a large paved terrace surrounded by garden beds. I was initially responsible for planting these gardens but knew that the eventual owners would alter the planting schemes to suit themselves and that this would create an unavoidable element of inconsistency along the

OPPOSITE *These date palms at the Anchorage were planted with the help of a huge mobile crane. The trees were deliberately chosen with bent trunks so that they would lean over the terrace, creating a natural effect and providing a sense of animation.*

[94]

façade of the building. However, between these private gardens and the seashore I decided to use plants that would be ecologically compatible with the indigenous ones. Here I planted large clumps of lavender, rosemary, *Felicia amelloides*, valerian, teucrium, broom, myrtle, echium and gazania, as well as succulents such as aloe and mesembryanthemum.

The influence of the sea and its salt spray created a series of different natural habitats on the site. The two- to three-metre-high cliffs on which the apartments were built fell into the bay. This bay was protected from the open sea by an island several hundred metres offshore, on which stood a ruined medieval tower. The western end of the building extended almost to the end of a short peninsula. At this point the island gave little protection, and the winter gales occasionally sent waves crashing over the rocks. It was a harsh maritime environment, and the land here was almost bare of soil and vegetation.

Various local nurserymen said that it would be impossible to get any plants to thrive here. They would always look windswept and half dead. Disheartened but not entirely without hope, I sent off to Australia for

sea rosemary, *Westringia fruticosa*, which is a maritime plant with grey foliage, and a variety of hibiscus called 'Apricot Beauty'. These arrived as tiny, vulnerable plants, but fortunately their new surroundings appealed to them and they thrived, just as they do on the harsh edges of the Pacific Ocean in Sydney. I also planted the native atriplex here.

Unfortunately, in my haste to prove that I could get plants to grow in this hostile setting, I forgot one of my cardinal rules. Westringia and hibiscus are ecologically incompatible. The former likes dry conditions whereas the other likes a far more humid soil. When planted together, despite the fact that they both flourished, they looked like chalk and cheese. As a result, this end of the garden is the only part of the development for which I was responsible that has a confused and unresolved appearance. Other plants used in the more protected parts of this exposed maritime zone and which are ideally suited to the site were *Pittosporum tobira* and the New Zealand Christmas tree, *Metrosideros excelsus*.

ABOVE *A small island close to the shore creates a sheltered bay in front of the Anchorage and helps protect its gardens from salt spray in the winter storms.*

Our main task at the Anchorage was to create an atmosphere of glamour that would attract the attention of the whole of Europe. Majorca had previously had the reputation of being a resort for package tourists, and very few of the hotels on the island to date could have been considered luxurious. But the Anchorage bravely set out to change the image of the island and, in the end, largely succeeded in doing so.

From the beginning I conceived of the Anchorage Club courtyard as an oasis: a paradise garden at the heart of the palace of some eastern potentate. Unfortunately, because the club's restaurant and bar opened onto the courtyard, there was a fierce competition for space during the design stages between revenue-earning tables and non-earning garden beds. Consequently, the scale of the garden beds in the courtyard was pared back.

I designed the courtyard garden from the vantage point of the flight of steps leading down from the building's main entrance. On this central axis is the swimming pool, creating the focal point of the courtyard. Since the sea and the island in the bay with its crumbling stone tower could be seen only through a narrow strip of pine forest, the one body of water did not unduly compete for attention with the other. Directly in

line with the pool I designed a large dance floor using polished Spanish marble. In the remaining space on either side would be the garden beds. What could be planted here to create the greatest possible dramatic impact in the available space?

Once again, I used subtropical plants to create the effect of an oasis. Since the terrace was separated from its Mediterranean environment by the walls of the courtyard as well as changes of level, I felt, as in the Rembels' garden, that I had a licence to create this sharp dichotomy.

However, the Anchorage gardens and particularly the central courtyard needed the addition of some further element, which would not only create a sense of excitement but also give the gardens the air of having been established a long time. There was only one answer to this in Spain: the date palm, *Phoenix dactylifera*.

The date palm is a native of the natural oases of North Africa and grows indigenously in Europe only on the plain south of Alicante, on the Spanish mainland. Despite Palma de Mallorca being named after its palms, it is said that these trees are not native but were introduced to the island by the Romans. Whether natives or not, date palms have an exotic aura, conjuring up images of not-too-distant oases in Algeria and Morocco.

I went to Alicante in search of palms. There, Irineo Lopez, a specialist grower, agreed to sell me a large

number at wholesale prices. Date palms grow slowly, at approximately one metre a decade, and Lopez told me that the palms he would be selling me had been planted by his grandfather. He said that, likewise, he was planting palm trees for his grandchildren and great-grandchildren to sell one day.

Large date palms can be moved only in the summer, and to prepare them for transplanting they must have all their roots and most of their fronds cut off. Because the palms were to be transported by ship from Alicante to Palma I was limited to trees of *nueve metros de tronco* since the sea containers were nine metres long.

The day I went to Lopez's nursery to select the palms for the Anchorage is one I shall never forget, so fascinating was the task. Rather than have a series of palms with straight trunks, I wanted many to have individual characteristics which I could then exploit to create the right mood in the garden. I was able to buy one rare mature tree with three separate trunks, and another with two trunks. Several single-trunked trees were decidedly bowed, and these were needed so that I could lean them from the garden beds along the walls of the building and out over the club courtyard. The trees would give a certain amount of shade to anyone sitting below and, equally importantly, a sense of movement to my design.

Once the palm trees arrived in Palma, it took only a couple of hours to plant them in the courtyard with the aid of a large mobile crane. It was exciting work, pivoting and tilting the palms to create dramatic and unusual effects. Even though the trees were bare for the first couple of months – with only a few upright fronds remaining – the result was immediately transforming. The trees conferred a sense of age and belonging to the site, as though they had been growing there for nearly a century.

In the garden beds below the palms, we could now plant the large shrubs that Hugo Latymer and his nursery Hortus had been growing for us at Santa Maria for the previous two years. This, above all else, had to be an escapist garden, with shrubs in flower for as much of the year as possible.

'Most of the people who have bought apartments in the Anchorage are from northern Europe. When they arrive here from Hamburg or London we want them to be able to see and smell only those plants that grow in hot climates,' said my boss, Pat Samuel.

Huge hibiscus shrubs with pink and red flowers were eased into place, as were large banana trees. And in the tall narrow garden beds, which could dry out quickly, standard oleanders with bright-pink flowers were planted. Many of these shrubs were also placed in terra cotta pots which I had designed myself, and which had been made in a local

pottery. *Jasminum azoricum* climbed the courtyard walls – along with *Clematis armandii*, plumbago, with its sky-blue flowers, and star jasmine, *Trachelospermum jasminoides.*

The Anchorage's opening night party in September 1985 was the event of the year in Palma. And, happily, the gardens already had an air of maturity about them for the occasion.

ABOVE *Between the Anchorage and the sea the garden beds – representing different habitats – had to merge as seamlessly as possible. On the right, drought-tolerant New Zealand flax and the indigenous palm, Chamaerops humilis, grow in beds that do not have automatic watering. Close by, in beds that are irrigated daily, grow plants such as Hibiscus 'Apricot Beauty' and date palms.*

a

LANDSCAPE

garden

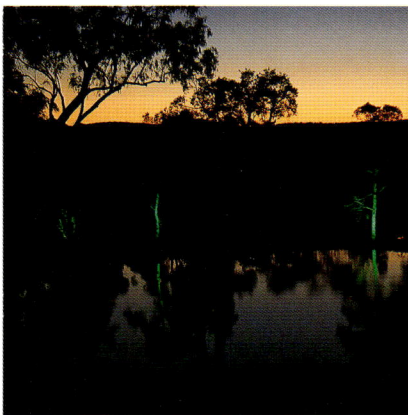

For seven years from January 1988, the landscaping of part of a large sheep and cattle station and its polo fields was to dominate my life. This station, in the Upper Hunter Valley in New South Wales, is encircled to the east by the Barrington Tops mountain range and to the west by the Mount Royal range. Between these two ranges the intervening hills undulate, giving the impression, in certain light, of a choppy sea in a state of suspended animation.

There is a distinct rhythm to this succession of hills and valleys, and to the streams that pass through them. And it immediately suggests that any man-made landscape should adopt these same natural rhythms and merge with them in as informal a way as possible.

Until my first visit to the site, I had no idea of the scale of what was involved. The building of the station's infrastructure was in full swing and would remain so for several years. My client and I arrived by helicopter and before landing did an aerial tour of inspection. The polo fields had just been sown with grass; the stables and various houses were under construction. Each of these disparate elements, scattered over many square kilometres, needed to be individually landscaped. And yet the whole needed to hang together as a unity and this would be the hardest task of all. It was an immense challenge.

My first job was to get to know the nature of the place and its native vegetation. Every worthwhile garden or park has an air of inevitability. And wishing to give this future park such a sense of belonging to its surroundings, it followed that the site itself had to dictate the way in which it should be landscaped.

Several images stored in my mind from that initial visit were instrumental in allowing me to do this. Perhaps the most important of these was that of the strong contrast that existed between the dry hills, where yellow box gum trees are dominant, and the narrow green valley floor, where streams and alluvial soil support ribbon gums, angophoras and casuarinas. Another enduring image was that of a waterfall, tumbling out of the mountainside of the Barrington Tops like a fragile bright ribbon, animating a dark background of gum trees. Yet another was that of Sargent's Gap to the west, in the Mount Royal mountain range. Here, haphazard groves of white box gum trees create a canopy over the winding dusty road, creating something of the mood of the Vale of Thermopylae in Greece.

Whatever we did had of necessity to blend well with these natural surroundings. The resulting landscape needed a sense of cohesion, and yet it had to change character from one place to the next in order to create interest. My client's most urgent imperative was that there be no walls in the landscape. 'I want the eye to be able to run unhindered to the horizon,' he said. As we discussed the important issues, a plan began to form in my mind.

Informal copses of both indigenous and exotic trees would be planted to create an Australian landscape garden, the scale of which would match those of eighteenth-century Europe. These plantations would be used to frame buildings and natural elements in the landscape, such as mountains and tall hills. They would also perform the practical tasks of providing shade and protection from the wind.

[102]

Here and there, as if in acknowledgement of mankind's staccato intrusion into the landscape and according with my style of design, there would be occasional formal plantings. As usual, I would use formality as a tool to link one area to another, usually by means of avenues of trees. Avenues might frame an informal group of willow trees leaning over a river crossing, but there would never be formality along the streams themselves.

Irrespective of the presence of water, I wanted to use avenues to frame copses of more natural appearance, since juxtaposing the two creates an exciting tension. Such compositions are always more effective when a distinct wedge of sunlight marks the space where an avenue ends and the shade of a copse begins. These contrasts of light and shade — and of masses and voids — are helpful tools in creating an interesting result.

The landscape I was asked to design and develop essentially followed the valley floor of two rivers upstream from their junction, in front of the station homestead, as well as for a considerable distance downstream. These water courses created an irresistible focal point. Both streams — Pages Creek and the Upper Hunter River — are narrow and, for the most part, have carved themselves deep beds. Consequently, it is rare to see moving water unless actually standing on their banks. This made it all the more imperative to suggest the presence of water by the

PREVIOUS PAGES *From the homestead garden a nearby hill, Mount Fairlight, is framed by* Eucalyptus melliodora *trees and reflected in a small lake. Seen in silhouette beneath the trees is the rose garden with its metal arches and Victorian fountain.* BELOW *The homestead garden and its lake seen from the air. The waterfall sits on the edge of the narrow upper end of the lake. Closer to the house is the oval-shaped rose garden.*

types of trees used. We undertook massive plantings of indigenous ribbon gums, *Eucalyptus viminalis*, which grow into splendid trees of immense height. To the initiated they signal the presence of alluvial soil and water. We also planted large numbers of exotic poplars and willows.

Of all the trees, the cottonwood poplars grew the most quickly once they got their roots into the watertable. I was particularly taken by the effect the sunlight had when filtered through their leaves, resulting in a greenish, cool light. As a result, I planted them in tight copses at several of the river crossings. On coming from the glare of the hills to the valley floor on hot summer days, the relief to one's senses from the sight and sound of water is heightened by the conditioned light of their dappled shade.

In early February 1990, before a copse of cottonwood poplars at one of the river crossings had a chance to establish itself, a flash flood swept many trees downstream. These had to be retrieved – some from a great distance – and replanted. Unbelievably, six days later, a worse flood struck and swept them away again. Once again, we replanted those that could be salvaged, and replaced the others. Fortunately, the trees were then able to establish themselves before the next major flood two years later. They will always remain vulnerable, however, to the damage caused by collision with large logs being borne downstream in a flood. But this is simply one of the hazards of planting trees on an ambitious scale in the Australian bush.

In addition to landscaping the station's water courses, our first priority was to plant trees around the polo fields. Apart from aesthetic considerations, the practical purpose of these trees is to provide shade, both for the tethered ponies waiting to be used in chukkas, and for spectators and their cars. On hot summer days, each polo field turns into an immense pool of sunlight, and it was important to plant quite densely in order

PREVIOUS PAGES *Large numbers of exotic trees have been planted close to the house for the cool of their shade in summer. On the left is a small group of London plane trees, particularly good for this purpose. On the right is a flowering* Prunus *'Ukon'.* ABOVE *Four concentric circles of* Paulownia fortunei × *'Powton' surround the exercise track on which polo ponies are exercised daily. Inside the one-kilometre-long exercise track are two islands and a lake, which has become a bird sanctuary.*

to create the necessary contrast of light and shade. In certain places I also designed straight rows of trees which were interspersed amongst more natural copses, as this formality married well with the structured nature of the fields themselves.

It was important that each of the polo fields should have its own distinct character. Around one, which was surrounded by an indigenous forest of *Eucalyptus melliodora* and *Angophora floribunda*, we planted principally exotic trees that wove in and out of the indigenous flora. Here we introduced a large copse of *Magnolia grandiflora* trees, which we planted in the lee of a hill to protect it from westerly winds. Deodars, tulip trees, Italian cypresses and elms were also planted in bold homogenous groups.

Around another field I derived much pleasure from composing a scheme of many different types of willows and poplars, which again we planted in large uniform drifts. To act as a foil and anchor to these visually light trees, I also used oriental plane trees and umbrella pines, *Pinus pinea*, which lent essential weight to the scheme.

In general, all the copses were planted in large homogenous groups — sometimes using up to fifty trees in each — not only because this often occurs in nature, but also to give the design a clarity and sense of purpose. Nothing is worse than amorphous groups of mixed trees that lack any distinct character because the designer is afraid to make a bold statement. Since the scale of the entire estate is so large, this kind of clarity is essential because the design needs to be read clearly across the length of a polo field, as well as from opposing hills.

Rather than designing the plantations on paper, where it was easy to confuse the scale and hard to take into account existing indigenous trees, which were always given precedence in my schemes, I worked almost entirely on site. Steel star-picket fence posts, as their name suggests, are usually used in the making of fences. I found them extremely useful as stakes to designate the location of future trees.

As always, it was important when orchestrating these plantations not to forget the role that time would

[*107*]

play in the scheme of things. By imagining the trees as mature specimens, I could then examine the effect of what I had designed from all angles. It was particularly important in the informal copses that the trees did not inadvertently line up with each other, as this looks unnatural. The backhoe drivers and those who assisted with the planting quickly became adept at ensuring that this never occurred, even between neighbouring copses.

Because polo fields need to be irrigated with large quantities of water, we had an excuse to build several lakes, all the while pretending that their purpose was ornamental and not practical. These lakes, partially open to the surrounding landscape and partially protected from the wind by trees, have become bird sanctuaries. It is not uncommon to see flocks of migrating birds resting on the water including, one day, a group of pelicans driven inland by coastal storms. The presence of such large still bodies of water in the landscape of inland Australia has all the visual and emotive power of an oasis in a dry climate.

One of these lakes lies at the centre of a circular track of one kilometre's length where the polo ponies are taken and exercised each day. The lake has two islands and here we planted swamp cypresses, *Taxodium distichum*. These, however, have been slow to grow. Part of the problem is that the surface of the lake fluctuates according to the demand for water, and the roots of the trees sometimes become too dry. More successful have been the oaks, poplars, Italian cypresses, umbrella pines and pussy willows. Because the area encircled by the exercise track is isolated from the broader landscape beyond, I felt inspired to create a miniature, inward-looking, heroic landscape not unlike parts of Centennial Park in Sydney and the Borghese Gardens in Rome.

To give the horses shade whilst being exercised, we decided to plant a very decorative cultivar of paulownia called 'Powton', around the track. Four concentric rings of these trees were planted, two rings on the inside and two on the outside: a total of more than 360 trees. Despite assurances to the contrary, they were, whilst young, vulnerable to drought, flood, frost and hot winds, all of which the local climate was capable of providing in abundance. Many of the small trees died and had to be replaced. One of the great advantages of paulownias, however, is that they grow extremely quickly, and within seven years they were already semi-mature. The spectacle of them in full flower in spring made up for the initial problems. When approaching the station by air in early October, you can see the trees as a pink furze from a distance of fifty kilometres or more.

Of all the exotic trees we planted on the station, Chinese elms, *Ulmus parvifolia*, were the single greatest success. Not only do these trees grow reasonably quickly, but they tolerate droughts well and give good protection from the wind. As a result we planted more Chinese elms than any other single exotic tree.

The second most successful exotic tree we used was probably the Manchurian pear, *Pyrus ussuriensis*. With age this becomes quite a large and handsome tree with attractive foliage and flowers. Its survival can be perilous for the first season after it is planted, but once established it is remarkably drought- and wind-tolerant for a tree of such fragile beauty.

Machinery has made the creation of landscapes on this scale much easier. Whereas in eighteenth-century Europe a cheap and skilled labour force existed literally to sculpt the land by hand, in the late twentieth century there are bulldozers, excavators, backhoes and helicopters. I once spent a rainy winter's morning in the attic library at Longleat, reading the original handwritten contracts between Capability Brown and Lord Weymouth. It was fascinating to read about how many hours of hard manual labour — and how many labourers, horses and drays — were needed to landscape such a park extending over hundreds of hectares.

Whilst it is now possible to create machine-made landscapes extremely rapidly, it is still essential, if the land is to be well sculpted, for the final levelling to be done by hand. To put the finishing touches to a newly

OPPOSITE *Groups of cottonwood poplars were planted at many of the river crossings in order to emphasise the presence of water and to condition the sunlight on hot summer days.*

[*108*]

created hill or the banks of a lake, a regiment of gardeners armed with rakes is still the only way to create the best possible effect.

Nevertheless, mechanical aid was invaluable in creating the station's landscapes: in making its lakes as well as the occasional hill, and planting its thousands of trees. In the winter of 1988, we started and finished planting an entire avenue of claret ash in just one day. A backhoe dug the holes in the morning, and a helicopter delivered the trees from our holding nursery to each of the holes in the afternoon. Modern technology would prove essential, too, in creating the heart of this landscape park, the homestead garden.

On first visiting the homestead, perched on its own hill directly above the Upper Hunter River — at this point, still actually a stream — I was immediately aware of the presence of water and yet was unable to see it. And while much of the homestead's garden was on a steep slope falling towards the water, my concern was that it lacked focus.

The main façade of the house faced west and overlooked a large field that sat on a broad bend of the Upper Hunter River. This open and level space resembled an oval and reminded me of certain paintings by John Firth-Smith. The more I thought about it the more a lake suggested itself to me, and I was reminded of and inspired by the lake that Dame Elisabeth Murdoch had created at Cruden Farm near Melbourne the previous year.

Once suggested to my clients the idea of a lake was adopted with alacrity. Using a bag of plaster, I poured out its proposed outline and over the following twelve months it became a reality. We discovered that the soil in which the lake was dug was so alluvial, with such a marked absence of clay, that we had to line the entire bed of the lake with black plastic in order to retain the water. This plastic lining was so thick that its seams were welded together as if it were metal.

Initially it bothered me that a lake, which I had intended to resemble a natural lagoon in the bend of the river should, by virtue of its plastic lining, look so artificial. However, we dug the lake so deep that the plastic was only visible in the shallow areas near the edge, and very soon this too disappeared as natural algae covered the bottom. Finally, by allowing natural grass and rushes to grow on the verge of the lake and into the water itself, we completely disguised the plastic. After a year's growth it was impossible to tell that the lake was lined at all.

At the far end of this lake, at its narrowest point, I constructed a waterfall using the largest and most attractive boulders I could find on the station. I searched for them by helicopter and then went to inspect them on the ground in a four-wheel-drive utility truck. Some of them were in remote valleys where access was difficult. Eventually these rocks were lifted onto several lorries by bulldozer, and delivered to the site. We hired a large mobile crane and started the painstaking work of construction.

The water supply for the waterfall comes from a dam on the hill behind the homestead, the volume of which is controlled by a valve. When the valve is fully open, 4000 litres of water a minute passes over the waterfall. From the homestead lake the water is then pumped to another artificial lake before being used to irrigate the polo fields.

Despite being constructed of natural stone and being sited on the steepest, and hence topographically most realistic, part of the lake, the waterfall looked artificial once completed. It needed to be blended into the landscape. I wished to create a tree-fern forest similar to those naturally occurring near waterfalls in the nearby mountain gullies. But first we needed to establish a microclimate to give this forest the protection it required

Opposite *The earth dug up in the construction of the lake at the centre of the exercise track was used to create islands and a small hill at its western end.*

PREVIOUS PAGES *This waterfall was designed and constructed at the narrow end of the lake. A small forest was created so that its surrounding groves of tree ferns would survive the summer sun and winter frosts. Indigenous bullrushes were then added to the verge of the lake.* ABOVE *Rocks were introduced to the garden and buried in the Japanese tradition. Most of the tree ferns, Dicksonia antarctica, were tilted in a drunken fashion since this is the way they grow naturally.* OPPOSITE TOP *Stepped garden beds were created on a rocky bank at the entrance to the homestead garden. Yellow-and-orange-flowering kniphofias and day lilies were planted to blend with the foliage of the golden elms in the background.* OPPOSITE BOTTOM *A moist pocket of the rose garden, where the water from the automatic irrigation system drains slowly, gave us the excuse to plant Japanese water iris, Iris kaempferi. When not in flower, its foliage creates a pleasing effect.*

from the hot summer winds, winter frost and harsh sunlight. Starting the winter after the waterfall was completed, we planted great numbers of *Angophora floribunda* trees, and wattles. Within three years these trees were large enough to provide the necessary canopy and we could start planting tree ferns. We used *Dicksonia antarctica* and various kinds of cyathea including my favourite, *Cyathea cooperi*, with its pock-marked trunks.

For the first few years these tree ferns were badly hit by frost, despite being sheltered by the trees. By the time spring arrived they would be totally bereft of fronds, which would then take several months to regrow. As the years passed, however, the canopy of gum trees and wattles gave increased protection. We also learnt that some pockets of this man-made habitat were warmer than others. Since the cyatheas are more vulnerable to frost than the dicksonias, we moved them into these milder areas. Although it took years, the creation of this tree-fern forest is one of my most worthwhile struggles in this garden.

Meanwhile, the landscape around the lake continued to throw up additional challenges. We found that swamps were being created close to the waterfall and the tree-fern forest as a result of excess water from the automatic irrigation system used to water the homestead lawns. My client had the idea of converting these swamps into beds of water iris. I was initially dubious since the first beds were small and would look

imposed upon the landscape. But the water iris grew extremely well, and the beds were expanded to such immense proportions, that I must now say my early reservations were ill-founded. Moreover, the groups of water iris and tree ferns complement each other perfectly.

The surroundings of the lake and waterfall are planted with local native trees to create an idealised, wild Australian landscape. I was interested to see how the decision to use only indigenous trees around the lake worked. It meant that the new plantations blended with the existing self-sown ones, which in turn has lent the lake and waterfall a powerful sense of belonging. In creating such seemingly natural effects, I am reminded that the art of landscape design is the art of sleight-of-hand.

This landscape, with the lake and waterfall at its centre, was designed as the main focal point of the homestead garden. Around the house itself are yellow box gum trees mixed with exotic trees. Since yellow box trees have comparatively tall and open crowns, they are not tremendously effective in providing shade and protection from the wind during the summer months. In contrast, such exotics as planes, ashes, *Magnolia grandiflora* and Manchurian pears perform this function well, and we have used many of them for this reason.

In the cool and shady environment that has resulted, a large number of wide garden beds have been added to those that originally

OPPOSITE TOP LEFT *Contrasting foliage is more important in herbaceous and shrub border design than flower colour. Here a flowering Hydrangea quercifolia is surrounded by the foliage of sedum, crassula and stachys.* OPPOSITE TOP RIGHT *The towering spires of Salvia turkestanica in flower create a dramatic effect in one of the shrub borders. Salvias have a tendency, however, to self-seed and to shade other perennials out of existence.* OPPOSITE BOTTOM RIGHT *The foliage of stachys, lavender and Koelreuteria paniculata — a small tree with yellow flowers — contrast with the viburnum on the right of the picture.* OPPOSITE BOTTOM LEFT *The leathery, sculptural foliage of* Viburnum rhytidophyllum *is used as a foil against which other plants provide interesting variations. In this instance,* Salvia forsskaolii, *flag iris and phlox have been used.* ABOVE *Pinks, mauves and blues work well in the rose garden. Here the pink-flowering rose 'Comte de Chambord' is surrounded by spiked speedwell,* Veronica spicata *'Blue Spires', the flowers of which appear both mauve and blue in dappled sunlight.*

[*117*]

existed around the house. The various beds have different themes. One, for example, is a bed of *Magnolia soulangeana* and tree camellias, *Camellia reticulata*. These trees provide extra shade for an entire wing of the house, including the kitchen. They are underplanted with large numbers of spring bulbs, anemones and primulas so as to give a continuous display of colour from September until late November.

Another bed has as its main theme Japanese maples underplanted with dwarf maples. Bill Seal, a highly original and talented gardener, gradually took over the design of most of the garden beds around the homestead since I was preoccupied designing plantations of trees. With the client, we would discuss the layout of each of the beds at length, and tell each other how we saw each bed developing. But with time, we were increasingly happy to leave many of the beds more or less entirely in Bill's hands.

In 1992 I designed a new rose garden for the homestead garden. As a point of departure, I took as my inspiration the circular rose garden at Boughton House in Northamptonshire with its concentric rings of flower beds and lawns. In the end, however, we were unable to create a circular rose garden since there were too many mature trees on the lawn. The only way we could fit the rose garden into its chosen site without felling trees was to make it rectangular or oval.

We decided to make it oval, and to place a pond and fountain at its centre. Because we wanted the rose garden to be very enclosed, we decided to encircle it with large metal hoops bedded in concrete foundations. These hoops provide the supports on which the climbing roses grow.

Such an elaborately formal rose garden is not without an element of fantasy. Not dissimilar in spirit to the Duchess's rose garden in *Alice in Wonderland*, it threatened to look absurdly out of place and imposed if seen in its entirety in the wider context of the Australian bushland. It needed to be at least partially concealed from view in order to tone down its formality. I had noticed that escallonia grew particularly well in a garden bed next to the homestead and recommended it as a hedge to enclose the rose garden. It has proved to be very fast-growing, and has the bonus of having pink flowers over many months of the year.

The purpose of the rose garden was to cultivate both modern and old-fashioned shrub roses, and climbers. We also planted many floribundas like 'Iceberg', and hybrid teas like 'Savoy Hotel' and 'Just Joey'. Amongst the roses, and acting as a foil, are herbaceous perennials such as salvias, lavenders, sedums, veronicas, irises and epimediums. I have attempted to limit the flower colours of these perennials to pink, white, blue and mauve since these colours accord best with the roses, the predominant colours of which are pink, cream and apricot.

The rose garden is strategically sited to link various garden beds and plantations on the northern side of the homestead with the lake to

PREVIOUS PAGES *The rose garden was designed as a secret garden in which an abundance of water and scented flowers contrast with the dry slopes of Mount Fairlight in the background. In the mid-ground is a glimpse of the homestead lake.* OPPOSITE *To enhance the sense of enclosure in the rose garden, metal arches were designed on which to grow climbing roses. The climbing rose on the left is 'Black Boy'; in the foreground the pink flowers of 'Chaucer' rise from a groundcover of Santolina pinnata 'Edward Bowles'.*

the west. Before the rose garden existed, this side of the garden lacked cohesion. But the importance of the rose garden – and other formal elements in the wider landscape such as the exercise track – goes beyond that. They have been designed as a counterpoint to the general theme. In such an immense and ultimately open landscape, their intimate scale and inward-looking character reassuringly envelop the human frame, whilst their geometry evinces the hand of mankind in a landscape that otherwise pretends to be natural and wild.

In the end, we planted more than 12 000 trees on the station. The majority were native gum trees, some of which came from the Forestry Commission in Muswellbrook. But we discovered in time that plants germinated from the seed of local native trees grew best of all.

The work I did in the Upper Hunter Valley was certainly the most complicated project of my career and one of the most challenging. What is most exciting now is that, thanks to excellent maintenance and regular watering, the effect we wished to create is becoming a reality as the trees start to mature.

OPPOSITE *When it was designed on paper, the rose garden had a strict symmetry and straight paths. That severity has now been relaxed, with groundcover plants claiming a large portion of the paths and forcing visitors to wend their way amongst them.*

a COURTYARD *garden*

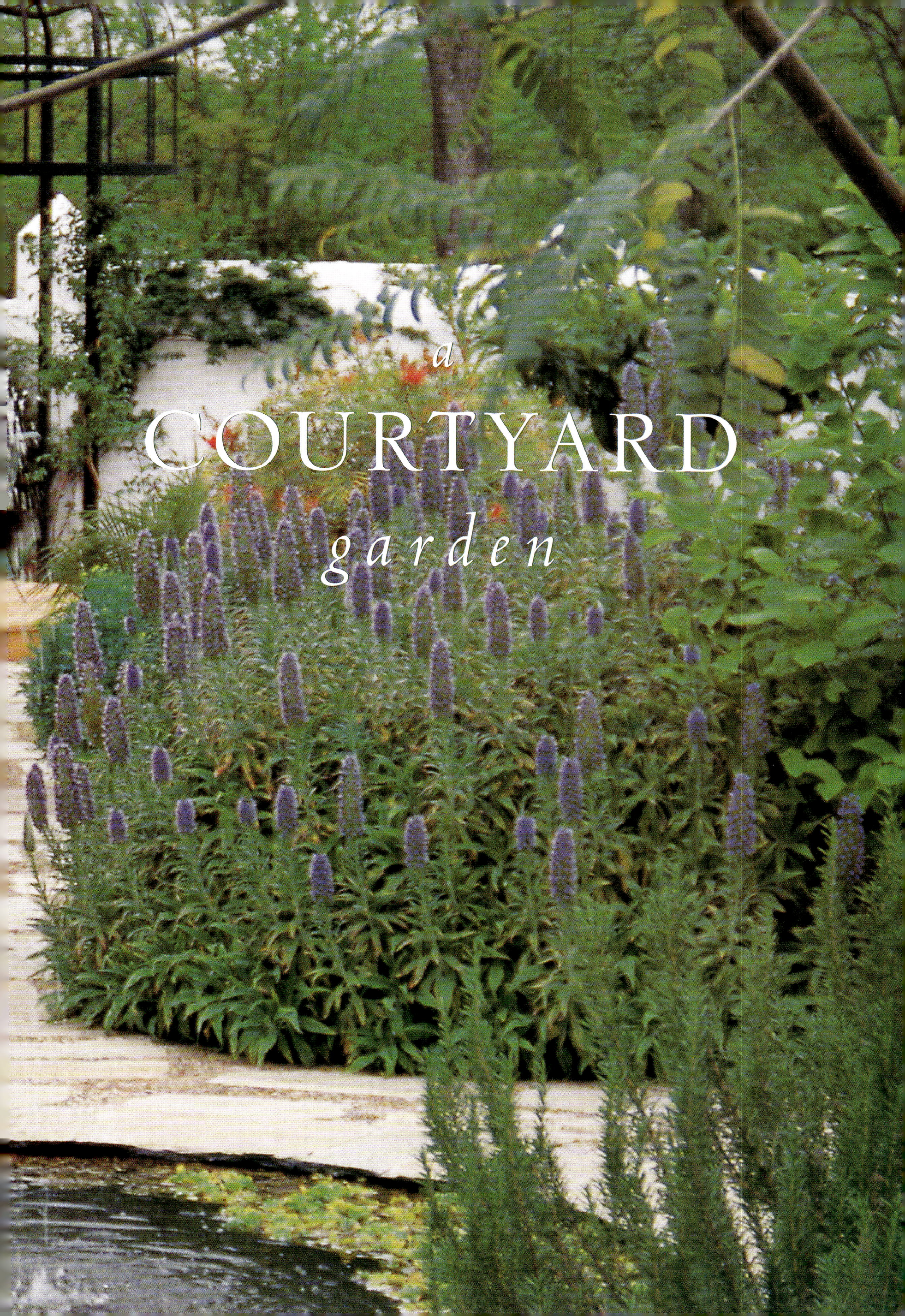

Needing inspiration for a garden I was designing on the west coast of Scotland, I decided to visit another part of the world with similar conditions of high rainfall and acid soil, and where the native flora was very interesting. That Easter I travelled to Patagonia – in both Argentina and Chile. There I saw eucryphias with flowers as wide as plates and five different species of nothofagus at the peak of their autumn colour. I also saw crinodendrons, Myrtus apiculata and many other plants that might suit the Scottish garden.

During my visit, I was invited to stay on an *estancia*, or ranch, in the foothills of the Andes. Whilst there, my host told me that he was building a new house on a sporting estate in Uruguay which had several kilometres of river frontage. The new house was to have a large courtyard. Would I design a formal garden for him there? Since I was pressed for time, it was decided that I would start designing the garden from plans and photographs in London, and return to South America to visit the site six months later.

It was one of the few occasions in my life that I began a project without first visiting the site. It can be a dangerous thing to do since there will almost always be a surprise; a factor that you didn't foresee and which no one else felt was significant enough to mention. It might be some man-made horror. On the other hand, it might be something subtle and wonderful in the view that needs to be drawn into the garden. In this case, however, there were no surprises. The house was definitely the focal point of the courtyard, and the surrounding native forest of trees and dense shrubs was unremarkable.

The house, which was still being built, had been designed by Joel Petit de la Villeon of Montevideo. It was situated on a low rise, looking west over the Uruguay River. Its courtyard emerged from the base of a tower from which the two wings of the house extended south and north. This ensured that most rooms enjoyed views onto both the river and the future courtyard garden. Because the ground sloped away gently, the northern end of the house dropped down a metre and a half, and here the architect had located the garage and staff quarters. But the change in level also cut short the northern part of the courtyard.

The focal point of the entire courtyard was the tower. The front door of the house was located here, and the tower served as the notional centre of the house. Furthermore, the deepest part of the courtyard was directly opposite this point. More than anything else, this central axis made the tower's importance to any future garden unassailable. The main problem was that having decided to centre the garden along the principle axial line, the northern end was approximately half the area of the southern end.

My client had requested a formal garden, necessitating clearly delineated axial lines and symmetry. But the geometry with which I was presented was noncompliant. No matter how I played with it, I was unable to create a symmetrical garden. I thought of Russell Page and how he turned asymmetry to great advantage when designing formal gardens. In the end, he invariably manipulated the site in a convincing way.

On his death in 1985, Russell Page left all his garden plans to Robert and Jelena de Belder in Belgium. I once spent a winter's weekend as the de Belders' guest at Kalmthout Arboretum going through them. I learnt far more that cold and windy weekend than I expected. Russell Page, being a master, knew how to placate, if not deceive, the eye. He understood the extent to which he could strain the limits in creating a sense of formality in seemingly impossible situations.

Above all, he understood the degree to which the human eye is predisposed to accept certain forms as being symmetrical. And he knew that the eye would only question apparent symmetry if given good reason to do so. The important issue is not what the plan looks like on paper, nor what the bird's-eye view might be. Instead, the designer must exploit the rules of perspective and the limitations of human stature. Once again the landscape designer becomes a conjurer.

Putting the question of symmetry briefly to one side, I focused on the general shape and feel of the courtyard, making an early decision to increase its depth and to enclose it completely within garden walls. These walls were to be high enough to give the garden a sense of enclosure, and to hide the garage and staff quarters from view. By increasing the depth of the U-shaped courtyard I was able to take advantage of the natural terrain and make the bottom of the garden one metre lower than the rest. Here I suggested that we make a very small but totally separate garden to give the courtyard an air of mystery and surprise.

PREVIOUS PAGES *A courtyard garden, particularly in a warm climate, is brought to life and given a sense of coolness with the sight and sound of falling water. The tree with the cable-like branches extending across the top of the picture is a Cassia alata.* BELOW *The house stands on the edge of a forest and overlooks the immense Rio Uruguay. The large circular pond to the left of the house is a tanque australiano, which supplies the house and garden with water pumped from the river.*

The first part of the design to be addressed was this far eastern end of the courtyard, which lay furthest from the house. By building a semicircular retaining wall to enclose this lower garden, a relatively symmetrical space could be created. I say *relatively* symmetrical simply because the courtyard walls would weave a little at this point, dodging certain attractive trees which grew outside its perimeter. In addition, the steps down to this small garden from the rest of the courtyard would not be at its centre. But it did not matter; indeed it lent a certain charm. The important issue was that they be on the principal axis of the upper courtyard garden, which led to the front door of the house.

On entering the lower garden, one would immediately experience a great sense of privacy. To exploit the situation further, I proposed that we turn the space into a secret garden, not only using large plants to hide its existence, but also giving it a separate character from the rest of the garden. In so doing we would be turning the geometry at this end of the courtyard to our advantage, since it would now look as if the steps entering the lower garden were purposely off-centre, thereby enhancing the sense of privacy.

To fully enclose the garden and give it the sense of secrecy we desired, I suggested a screen of bamboo, which we would place around the top of the semicircular retaining wall. And to give what we now refer to as the Secret Garden its own focus, a very simple, raised tank would be built against the centre of the end wall. Water would fall from a gargoyle on the wall into the tank, reinforcing the individuality of this part of the garden.

However, yet to be resolved was the design of the upper courtyard where one side of the garden was still almost twice the size of the other. Here I was committed to creating the impression of symmetry where there seemed to be little hope of successfully achieving it. I began by establishing what the focus of the garden would be. Once again, I chose water, and designed a circular pond with a single jet of water at the centre of the courtyard, along the principal axial line that ran from the front door to the steps of the Secret Garden.

Placing the pool in the middle of the garden seemed the right decision at first, particularly since it created a very strong cross-axis. But the strict right angles that resulted only served to accentuate the asymmetry of the courtyard. The effect was clumsy. The situation was very similar to the one I faced with the upper vegetable garden in Bloomfield Hills, Michigan. And, as in that case, initial progress was slow.

Finally, I decided that the circular pond should be located as close to the house as its scale would permit. The design problems then resolved themselves fairly quickly. By sliding the pool along the principal axial line towards the house, I was able to give the impression that the decision had

Previous pages Water is inescapably the most important feature of the Secret Garden, and to create a different sort of music from that being played by the jet in the circular pond, a gargoyle was placed on the garden wall. Above To give it a totally different character from the larger courtyard, subtropical plants were used in the Secret Garden.

been made of my own volition so as to create a greater intimacy between the house and the pond. It was gratifying to be able to turn an apparent disadvantage into something that works in one's favour.

Moreover, because the pool was the apparent centre of the garden without actually being so, the eye did not question the geometry of the six paths that radiated from it. On arriving at the main gate in the centre of the northern side of the courtyard, anyone entering the garden needed to take a path angled at forty-five degrees in order to reach the pond. Once at the pond, one turned 135 degrees to reach the front door of the house. On the other hand, the steps leading into the Secret Garden were located forty-five degrees in the opposite direction.

The eye would overlook these widely divergent angles. The important thing was that the six paths, representing three separate axial lines, converged on the pond before passing notionally through the water jet and continuing uninterrupted beyond. What would have been immediately queried was if any one of these three separate axial lines had not been absolutely dead straight and true to itself.

The existence of the circular pond and its jet of water had an additional role to play in this visual deception. Whenever water is introduced into a garden it will invariably capture one's attention before any other single element. The fact that in this garden the pond so convincingly claimed to mark the nominal centre of the courtyard helped win the case.

The major stumbling block, of course, was that each of the garden paths that radiated from it were of different lengths. Since one path, in particular, led to the largest corner of the garden, the asymmetry was still clumsily apparent on paper. This gave me cause for concern in finalising the design. There were two things I did to ameliorate the problem.

Firstly, I ended the path in question in a large gazebo which, because of its height and apparent mass, made this side of the garden appear smaller than it actually was. Secondly, I decided to plant each of the beds in an informal manner, striving nonetheless to balance the mass of one bed with another. Thus, using trees and shrubs to alternately conceal and reveal, I was able to edit what the eye saw in different parts of the garden.

Fortunately for garden designers, the eye can see only in one direction – and can fully focus only on one detail – at a time. Therefore, when one stood by the circular pond and looked along a path towards the main garden gate, and then turned and looked towards the gazebo along another, one's eye accepted these two focal points as being sufficiently equidistant not to call the issue into question.

Most of this design was thrashed out on paper, so by the time I arrived in Uruguay to see the site for the first time, the basic layout of the garden had been decided upon. Driving from Montevideo to Quebracho it was interesting to see the Uruguayan landscape for the first

ABOVE *There is something both improbable and ineffably luxuriant about the leaves of banana trees, particularly when used in a protected environment where they are neither burnt nor too tattered by the wind.*

time. It is flat country, gently undulating in places, in which it is still possible to see traditional white-painted cottages with thatched roofs. Its great distinguishing feature is the horizon.

Because the landscape is so level, the horizon is distant. You know immediately that you are in a remote and little-populated part of the world. Even as an Australian, albeit from the eastern seaboard, I am not entirely accustomed to landscapes where the human figure is diminished to almost complete insignificance. Even though we may not be aware of it, experiences like these are subconsciously unsettling. Under such circumstances, an antidote to infinity is required to restore our confidence in our own stature.

The site of the house, with its panoramic view of the wide Rio Uruguay beyond which lay Argentina, was remarkable. During the entire journey from Montevideo one does not get a glimpse of the river until the last one hundred metres, and after discussing the mechanics of arriving at the house, my client decided that the visitor should be further denied this view by planting it out.

Our reasoning was that from the car one would enter the courtyard garden on foot through the gate in the northern wall. It was hoped that passing through the garden would be a cathartic experience. After hours of exposure to an infinite horizon, the courtyard garden – with its reassuringly small scale, ordered layout, sense of enclosure, scent of flowers and sounds of splashing water – would restore the visitor's sense of perspective to a human scale. We felt such restoration to be necessary before entering the house and being presented with the surprisingly wide panorama of the river for the first time.

On my first visit to the site, the most important unanswered question was what plants to use. Although I normally use native plants and allow them to dictate which exotics are included, I did not feel constrained to do so in this case. This would be, after all, a courtyard garden enclosed from the reality of its surroundings. Under such circumstances I enjoy creating a stark contrast between the enclosed garden and the natural landscape beyond. Amongst those indigenous plants growing naturally in the surrounding woods there are jacarandas, herbaceous lantana and *Tipuana ipe*, a very large tree that produces flamboyant pink flowers in spring.

My client had known Charles, Vicomte de Noailles, in whose garden I had worked as a *stagiaire* in 1975. We had talked a lot about Monsieur de Noailles and in the back of my mind was the thought of planting the garden as a tribute to him. I thought of the Villa Noailles at Grasse and its interesting collection of plants with their surprising juxtapositions. I wanted to do something that might have made Monsieur de Noailles smile in recognition had he still been alive.

Shortly after arriving in Uruguay, whilst passing through the village of Arroyo Malo, I was attracted by the leaves of some banana and orange trees leaning over a garden fence. We stopped so I could see the small garden that lay behind. I discovered a small paradise garden which provided its owners with pleasant shade and scented flowers as well as food. What was more, there was an interesting haphazard formality to its design. 'This is your garden!' I said to my momentarily surprised client. I particularly liked the idea that not only did the garden provide fruit and culinary herbs, but that this intention was clearly apparent in its layout.

By the time I sat down and actually did a planting plan for the courtyard garden I was in Australia. Following Monsieur de Noailles's example, I went through gardening books looking for a point of departure. I finally settled on a photograph of the garden Russell Page had designed for Sir William Walton in Ischia. Here he had created a paradise garden with plants chosen from all over the world. The result is extraordinary, and yet despite the flamboyant way in which it is planted, one senses an important cohesion in the compatibility of all of the plants.

The following winter I returned to Uruguay. By this stage the house was structurally complete and we were able to stay there. The concrete foundations for the paths and the pond had been poured, and in accordance with my instructions there was no soil yet in any of the garden beds. Instead, each of the beds had been excavated and was empty to the depth of one metre. The reason was so that I could ensure the builders hadn't disposed of any of their surplus rubble in the beds. Furthermore, it allowed me to control the quality of soil that was used.

As it happened, the huge piles of soil that had been delivered to the exterior of the courtyard were too heavy in texture. To counteract this, large quantities of river sand were brought in and mixed with the soil to lighten it. In their haste to complete the job, the workmen introduced too much pure sand into one of the beds, which subsequently meant that only certain types of plant would grow there, since it dried out so quickly. Initially I was disconcerted by this, but came to look upon it as a felicitous accident for it meant that the bed developed its own subtle character. Such plants as *Echium fastuosum* and *Convolvulus cneorum*, as well as various succulents and acacia, thrived here, as did sea rosemary, *Westringia fruticosa*, an Australian plant that grows in dry sandy soil in its natural habitat.

Indeed, as a result of such mishaps, and the fact that some corners of the garden are cooler and shadier than others, each garden bed comprised a series of slightly differing habitats. Following the natural slant of the terrain, the courtyard garden – although raised above its original level – also tilts to the north, albeit at a less acute angle. Nonetheless there is enough of a slope for water to percolate through the soil and make the garden's northern end an altogether different habitat from its southern half. Here citrus trees, hibiscus and jasmine were planted. In the northwestern corner, where the soil is wettest of all, and where there is partial protection from the eaves of the house, I placed a fruiting banana tree which has subsequently flourished. Such protection was necessary since winter temperatures occasionally fall to as low as minus five degrees Centigrade.

For the most part, however, the character of this garden was determined by its South American, Mediterranean, Australian and Californian plants, all of which enjoyed reasonably dry conditions. Such plants included rosemary, lavender, ceanothus, *Grevillea* × 'Moonlight', valerian, *Spartium junceum*, myrtle and an Italian cypress.

The Secret Garden – presaged by its loose surrounding hedge of bamboo – had a totally different character. Here we created a miniature rainforest garden which, under the circumstances, seemed to be the greatest flight from reality in this part of Uruguay. In such a comparatively dry and open landscape it was pleasant to have one small corner of the garden that was completely cocooned from the outside world, and that felt cool and humid. The plants used in the Secret Garden included philodendrons, ligularias, alocasias, Australian tree ferns and mondo grass. Such plants required protection from both sun and wind, and needed a canopy under which to grow. How could I provide this instant shelter when none of the nurseries sold trees taller than a few metres at the very most?

The only way to get immediate shade was to use the builder's backhoe to uproot four indigenous trees from the surrounding forest, and plant them outside the garden wall so that their branches overhung the Secret Garden. The obvious and most attractive choice was *Jacaranda mimosifolia*, and I hoped that at least one of the four rudely transplanted trees would live. Everyone else doubted that even one would survive. Nonetheless, I was greatly encouraged by the fact that most of these jacarandas were shallow-rooted. And thanks to the great care that David Furtado, the head gardener, gave them over the following summer, all four survived and in doing so saved the Secret Garden.

The Secret Garden proved a great success and not only have the metal garden chairs here been regularly

used, but a hammock has been installed for afternoon siestas. As a garden designer nothing gives me greater pleasure than seeing clients, their family and friends enjoying gardens in this way.

The final part of the garden to be resolved was the paving in the courtyard garden. This is an important detail, and I always strive for the greatest possible simplicity. Once again in this garden, it was a case of turning an apparent problem into an advantage.

Wanting to use a local stone, my hopes had been raised by the terraces and courtyard of a nearby *estancia*, La Favorita, which were paved in rectangular sawn slabs of subtly coloured rock. But La Favorita dated from the nineteenth century and the stone was no longer quarried. All we were able to find were roughly hewn slabs of limestone that would make crazy paving.

Disappointed by our lack of options, I later realised that such paving had advantages. To begin with, almost all the stones were roughly rectangular. Moreover, their colour was interesting and contrasted happily with the silver and blue foliage of many of the plants we were using. Finally, the roughly textured grain of the stone gave it a curious energy and movement. There was something discreetly sculptural about it.

Laying twenty slabs out on the ground, I moved them around, testing their effect in different arrangements. Placed with the grain

ABOVE *This photograph was taken less than fifteen months after the garden was planted and demonstrates how quickly the plants grew here. In order to balance the overall design, it was important that the gazebo be large so as to make this end of the courtyard seem smaller than it actually is.*

running lengthwise, they made me think of silver salmon, all facing upstream, side by side. The stone would lend each of the paths a sense of movement, with the flow always running ahead. Only around the central pond was the flow forced to eddy in a perpetual circle.

The secret to the success of the scheme was going to depend upon making certain that each stone 'floated' in enough concrete so that it could express its own character. This is what would finally give the paving its sculptural quality. It was important that the paving be laid whilst I was still in Uruguay so that I could oversee the placing of each stone. Ideally, the job should have been completed before the planting of the garden beds started. Unfortunately a good stonemason proved hard to find, and shortly thereafter the weather turned bad. It rained for several days whilst I contemplated the fact that I had appointments in Detroit and Perth that couldn't be delayed.

Finally, while the builders sat indoors refusing to venture out, I started to lay the first path myself. It was hard going, but by covering my work immediately with sheets of plastic, I was able to do a stretch of several metres, enough to serve as an example which could be followed by the stonemason after my departure. When I returned to Uruguay the following year, I saw that the mason had done a most reasonable job.

Even though I had initially envisaged this garden as being similar in spirit to Sir William Walton's garden in Ischia, the garden itself inevitably indicated the way it wished to go. I had imagined more sub-tropical plants, but these only thrived in the protected Secret Garden. It was the silver- and grey-foliaged plants that seemed, in general, to respond best to the climate in Uruguay. In fact they flourished with a vengeance. Moreover, several mimosa trees — and shrubs of santolina, artemisia, senecio, westringia and lavender — actually looked better with the stone paving than I had dared hope. On the other hand, old favourites such as daphne, wintersweet and *Bergenia cordifolia* sulked, and consequently were replaced with other plants. *Don't fight the site* is a very apt maxim.

Perhaps the most extraordinary phenomenon of all has been the speed at which this garden has grown. While this can be attributed in part to the pains taken in preparing the soil, it is also due to the fact that we didn't install an automatic watering system. Instead, David waters the garden by hand, giving each plant the individual attention it needs. In summer, the garden is watered every day. Then, just when the heat becomes almost unbearable, a *pampero* blows in from the south dropping inches of rain and cooling things down.

OPPOSITE *When covered with climbing plants — which are regularly pruned severely — the entrance pergola creates a pool of shade. The intention here was to give a pleasant sense of arrival, particularly since this is the main entrance to the garden through which the front door of the house is reached.* ABOVE *Easily the longest path in the garden is the one that extends from the gazebo back to the circular pond.*

a
NATIVE
garden

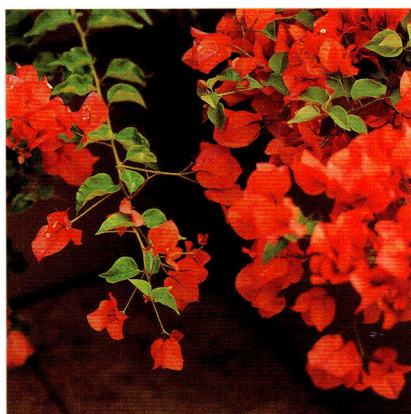

Four years ago, I was asked to advise on a site on the waterfront in Bayview, a northern suburb of Sydney looking down the length of Pittwater, a landlocked section of sea some thirty kilometres north of Sydney Harbour. On that first day the original house on the site was still standing. My clients, the Swains, told me that they were about to pull down the house and build a new one. Apart from other questions, they wanted to know what plants would grow in a garden with a northeasterly aspect onto Pittwater.

In answer to this I did what I always do, which is to make a list of those plants that are thriving with a similar aspect in neighbouring gardens. Such a list is an excellent starting point as further plants can later be added by inference. Fortunately, it was low tide and I was able to walk along the sand in front of nearby gardens. Amongst other things, I noticed that the cabbage tree palm, *Livistona australis* — a native palm tree of the Sydney region — thrived there.

It was nearly a year before I heard from the Swains again, but by that stage their new house was almost structurally complete. They were interested in landscaping the front garden as soon as possible. I returned to Pittwater to revisit the site. The change was extraordinary. The new house was three times larger than the bungalow it had replaced, yet it seemed to occupy less space. Part of the reason was that it had been built into the hill, with the swimming pool and gymnasium located underground. Yet despite being one storey down, the swimming pool looked up to the sky, thanks to a U-shaped retaining wall which, in effect, created a sunken courtyard.

The below-ground swimming pool, protected from the wind, was a sun trap, and it didn't require the mandatory ugly fence to prevent accidental drowning. Furthermore, the subterranean gymnasium in the house looked directly onto it. This imaginative design meant that the swimming pool did not intervene in one's view of the garden or the sea. Because of the unsettling quality of their hard edges and unnaturally clear water — often cast with electric hues — swimming pools are normally impossible to reconcile with the wider garden. And they are at their most discordant when built within sight of an interesting view.

Any body of water that is introduced to a garden will demand notice, and my garden designs draw strongly on the power of water to attract the attention over and above any other feature. To place a pool — or any body of water — between one's house and a compelling view is, in almost all circumstances, a blunder, simply because the eye will rove ceaselessly between pool and view without finding the subconscious rest it seeks. The more spectacular the panorama, and the brighter and larger the pool, the more this is the case.

PREVIOUS PAGES *The brief for this garden was to create something that 'felt like the garden of a holiday house'. The best way to achieve this was through utter simplicity in plant selection and the occasional discrete use of bright flower colour.* OPPOSITE *Cyathea cooperi is a tree fern that tolerates exposure to sun, wind and salt spray. In this garden they were under-planted with dark green alocasias with ebony-coloured stems.*

When the view in question is a large natural expanse of water such as the sea, the error is compounded. The comparatively small swimming pool will compete visually with the sea, the artificial colour of its water creating a jarring note. The effect is often absurd, as though a flashy minnow were attempting to compete with a whale, and the garden's relationship with the sea is immediately set awry.

As was the case here, I always urge that swimming pools be placed in their own walled or hedged spaces, where they can dominate their surroundings to their heart's content. A subterranean courtyard facing upwards towards the sky offered almost unparalleled liberties. This gave me complete licence to indulge in fantasy without having to face the consequences of possible incompatibility with the wider garden's sense of place.

Because this courtyard faced north it was an ideal spot to grow sub-tropical plants, such as bananas, in pots. The great attraction of banana plants is the unlikely shape, colour and texture of their leaves, which always manage to convey a delightful mood of fantasy. However, one of the problems with growing banana trees in Sydney is that their leaves become tatty and brown as a result of windy summers and cool winters. In this protected swimming-pool courtyard, these problems were minimised.

Directly above and parallel to the Swains' underground courtyard was a long and wide terrace that looked north over the entire length of Pittwater. From here, if one looked down, it was possible to see the swimming pool. However, a raised garden bed of thirty centimetres' width obscured the pool, directing the eye towards the sea instead. Very little space separated the Swains' house from their neighbour's, which was at a slightly higher elevation. Here a series of raised, narrow garden beds stepped up towards the boundary.

In front of the house, a broad, generous lawn sloped gently towards the sea wall. Because of the topography of the site, the eastern end of the lawn protruded further into the sea than the western end, where a boatshed and jetty stood. On this eastern side there were approximately ten metres of lawn between the house and the adjoining property. Furthermore, the neighbouring house was partially hidden by trees.

Sue Swain had done some research into the natural history of the site and discovered that cabbage tree palms had once been endemic. She had already decided that we must use them, a decision with which I happily concurred.

After Andrew Langford, the landscape contractor, had found mature specimens, we began planting cabbage tree palms in the raised garden beds on the western boundary of the house. We then extended the theme, and planted two small groups of palms on either side of the lawn, framing the house. They looked so good that we immediately

ABOVE *The most appealing qualities of* Cyathea cooperi *tree ferns are their parasol-like canopies, and the fine tracery of their leaves which creates a pleasant dappled shade.*

doubled the number, adding some smaller trees to make our groups look more natural. The effect of such bold and simple blocks of foliage – both on the front lawn and at the sides of the house – was visually exciting, whether seen from the main terrace of the house or from the sea.

Further planting was necessary to screen the house along its western boundary, and I recommended that we use another indigenous plant, *Cyathea cooperi*, the tree fern. This fern was a natural choice as it tolerates sun, wind and marine exposure. The huge advantage of *Cyathea cooperi* over the other well-known Australian tree fern, *Dicksonia antarctica*, is the delicate filigree of its fronds. *Dicksonia antarctica* is a plant of coarser appearance, and is less interesting in silhouette. Unlike the *Cyathea cooperi* it demands dappled shade, protection from winds and a humid atmosphere.

The only disadvantage of the tree fern is that for several weeks of the year it produces airborne seeds, which can become a nuisance if blown indoors. The Swains decided that they could cope with this minor inconvenience and so we planted some twenty tree ferns in the raised beds along the garden's western perimeter. Once again, the effect was so attractive that we immediately ordered more tree ferns for the eastern side of the house. We also leant some ferns over the sunken courtyard's retaining wall so that their strong sculptural lines could be seen from the swimming pool below.

Whilst the cabbage tree palms planted on the lawn required no further embellishment, those in the garden's raised beds needed a ground-cover plant. Apart from some small indigenous ferns, I recommended that we use alocasia – otherwise known as elephant's ears – for its small, finely shaped, dark copper leaves and stems. This created a powerful contrasting effect beneath the cabbage tree palms and tree ferns.

The retaining wall of the swimming-pool courtyard stood nearly two metres above ground level and needed softening. The Swains very much wanted the garden to convey the mood of a holiday house and this, we agreed, implied brightly coloured flowers. The panorama onto Pittwater was extremely broad and deep, and as a result the garden could take a certain amount of bright flower colour without it conflicting with the view. I recommended therefore that we plant a row of flamboyant hibiscus to hide the swimming-pool wall. These plants would be hidden from the house itself, and could be seen only when facing the house from the garden with one's back to the sea. The first row that we planted were *Hibiscus* × 'Pro Legato', but the flowers – instead of being the dark, velvet burgundy that we had seen growing in the nursery – were quite red. The reason for this, it was explained, was their exposure to the sea breeze. As a result, we replaced them with another variety, *Hibiscus* × 'Sunset Harvest', which have golden flowers that merge to orange, and these have proved a great success.

ABOVE *The swimming-pool courtyard is below ground level, creating a private, windless and sun-filled environment. Hanging from its raised planter box on the terrace above is* Bougainvillea × *'Glowing Sunset'.*

ABOVE *The view onto the sea is the most important element in this garden, and since the contest between a panoramic view and a garden is always an unequal one, the garden design was intentionally understated.*

We continued to use bright colours in the other garden beds that the architect had designed as part of the house. In the narrow raised bed that ran the length of the terrace, and which hid the swimming pool from view, we chose *Bougainvillea* × 'Glowing Sunset' because its orange flowers contrasted well with the hibiscus shrubs below. We also planted this on the upstairs terraces outside the bedrooms.

These boldly coloured exotic flowers are all grown in planter boxes which are part of the house and disassociated from the rest of the garden. The intention is that they be part of the immediate architecture, and not part of the reality of the broader landscape. They are there not only because they contrast well with the dun, earthen colour of the

house, but because they create a sense of excitement like flashes of light-
ning at night. In contrast to the fantastic quality of the plants growing
in the planter boxes, the largest and most conspicuous plants used in the
garden — the palm trees and tree ferns — represent reality. Because these
plants belong to the indigenous nature of the site they give the garden
its integrity and sense of place.

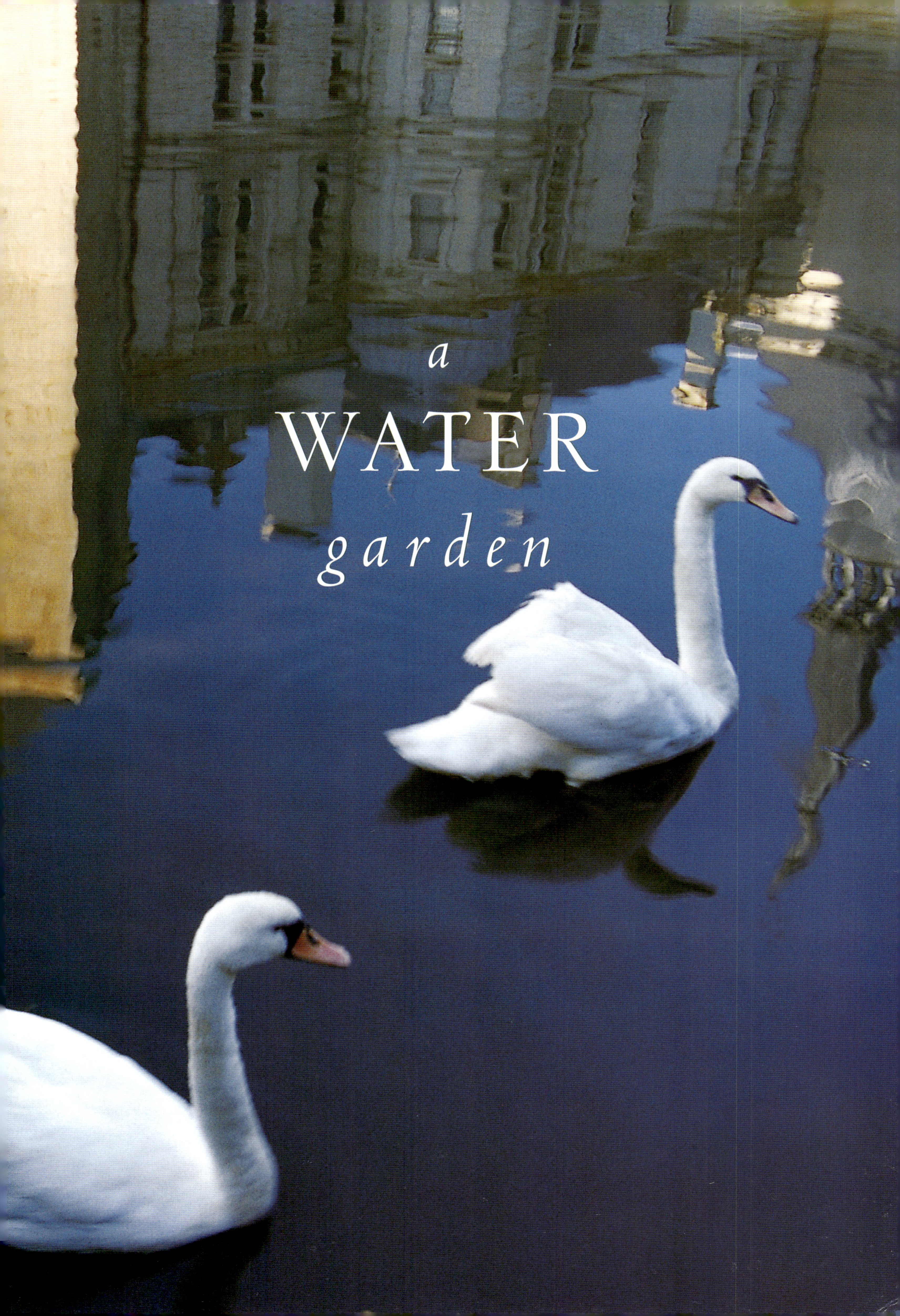
a
WATER
garden

I *first went to the Château de Sully on a hot and sunny day in May. Passing through the village, and turning through an imposing entrance, it was difficult to imagine a more romantic château in a more ideal setting. Seated on the floor of a wide valley, it is surrounded by water meadows and flanked by the River Drée. The remarkable stone carvings on the front parapet wall, the bridge leading across the moat to its entrance, and its large balustraded terrace with theatrically wide steps were vividly imprinted on my memory.*

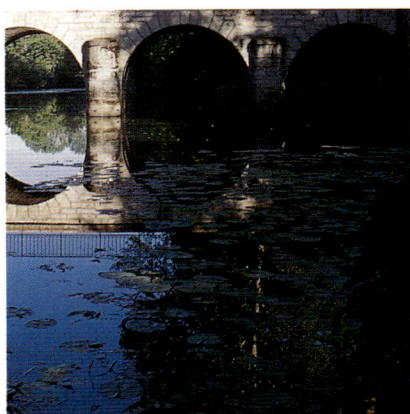

Few houses I have ever visited in the world have left such a strong impression. It was therefore with great pleasure that I accepted an invitation to advise on the restoration of its garden some nine years later.

The only garden I know in France with a similar charm to that of Sully is Courances, in the Île de France, south of Paris. Like Sully, the garden at Courances was probably designed by André le Nôtre in the seventeenth century, although the records are inconclusive. At Courances the soul of the garden is water and with sixteen springs within the park itself, as well as a stream, Courances is undoubtedly one of the greatest gardens in the world. What makes it so exceptional is that whilst it is grand, it is not overwhelmingly so. The scale is human and welcoming, and you don't feel swallowed up by the immensity of space. As a result of this, and the similarities of the two sites, the spirit of Courances has been my guiding star in planning the garden at Sully.

Like Courances, Sully is a garden of water. The sight of willows, poplars and alders growing along the edge of the River Drée signifies its presence. Then there are the deep reflections of the château and its arched bridge in the still water of the moat. Water is unquestionably the soul of the garden.

Quite different from the Château de Courances, the Château de Sully is built almost as a perfect square around a spectacular sixteenth-century internal courtyard. It is said that the site has been occupied since before Roman times. However, the château as it stands today is an interesting mixture of architectural elements. One of the four towers is said to date from the twelfth century, and its north front — which so impressed me on my first visit — from the eighteenth century. The west front is from the sixteenth century, and there are also elements that date from the nineteenth. For all that, Sully at first glance gives a splendidly medieval impression, as if an illustration from *Les Très Riches Heures du Duc de Berry* had suddenly come to life. It is not for nothing that Sully is nicknamed the Fontainebleau of the south.

Today Sully belongs to Philippe de MacMahon, fourth Duc de Magenta. The MacMahons, originally Wild Geese from Ireland, came to Sully by marriage in the eighteenth century. The present owner's great-grandfather was Maréchal MacMahon, victor of the Battle of Magenta in 1859, and later the first president of the Third

PREVIOUS PAGES *A family of swans brings life to the moat and stirs its reflections at Sully.* OPPOSITE *There is a magic about Sully — a château of simple grandeur — which comes from basic elements such as water, light, stone and time.*

[148]

ABOVE *In many respects the north front is the most important façade of the château and I would like it to be reflected in a lake to be constructed by widening the River Drée at this point.*

Republic. The present Duchesse de Magenta grew up in Scotland and, with extraordinary energy and capacity for hard work, she and her husband have embarked upon a long-term project to restore the garden.

When I first visited Sully parts of the garden resembled that of the castle of Sleeping Beauty. Briars and dog roses had thrived and impeded one's progress in certain directions. Maples, ash trees and conifers had also self-seeded and over the years grown tall.

Interestingly enough, when you arrive at Sully along the drive that leads to its west front, it is not until the last moment — as you cross the bridge to the front door of the château — that you become aware of the presence of water. The western side of the house, apart from its distant views onto the willows and poplars flanking the river, is quite *dry* in character: no natural or artificial bodies of water exist here. This slightly

teasing quality, of prolonging the visitor's discovery of the true character of the garden for as long as possible, is most appealing.

The south front of the house is also comparatively dry in character. Here, however, the moat is not tantalisingly hidden from view as it is on the western side. Looking back from the garden, you can see the château seated on its wide reflecting sheet of water. But apart from this view, there is no other water feature to be seen.

The views from both the eastern and northern sides of the house are quite different. Here water rules supreme. On the east front the eye is caught by a long, narrow canal. This approaches the château from a distance of one kilometre on its central axis and culminates in a rectangular pond, standing some seventy metres short of the moat in front of the house. On the north front, the River Drée comes quite close to the

house and – quite apart from the sight of its surrounding willows and alders – it is possible to see one of its ponds.

The Magentas and I decided that one of our first projects would be an immense program of clearing on the eastern side of the house to restore three separate vistas. The first vista would be a narrow one, its purpose being to give breathing space to the central canal which leads the eye to the trees, river and the low hills beyond. The second and third vistas would both be at forty-five-degree angles on either side of the canal, and would likewise lead the eye to the horizon.

The horizon is always crucial when designing gardens as it sets the mood more strongly than perhaps any other single quality. Whether it be formed by skyscrapers in New York or, as in the case of this perspective at Sully, a low wooded hill seen against the skyline, it determines the amount of sky that is potentially available to a garden. A high horizon gives a great sense of enclosure and can often seem forbidding. A very low horizon – with its concomitant feeling of infinite space – can also seem forbidding for opposite reasons. But in either case the garden designer must be aware of its influence and react accordingly.

Where the horizon is high and the garden already feels quite enclosed, I might be tempted to enhance this sense of enforced intimacy and enclose it further. At the same time, I must consider the result of my actions in all seasons of the year, as obviously the effect in summer will differ from that in winter. Alternatively, I may decide to fight the site a little, and admit as much sky into the garden as possible.

At Sully, the low wooded hills that define the horizon create a most relaxed mood. This encouraged us to make the two vistas on either side of the canal informal ones. Had André le Nôtre worked at Sully, as is suspected, he would have created formal *allées* along these axial lines and delineated them with avenues of trees. Such a design would seem logical given the existence of the formal canal and pond, and the initial temptation was to suggest it to the Magentas. But this would ultimately contradict the inherent pastoral qualities of the site as it currently stands and run counter to the genius of the place.

Perhaps if the horizon were lower, and if Sully didn't have its paradoxical sense of open intimacy, then dramatic formal vistas leading the eye into the open space would have created a sense of excitement. But whilst a degree of formality was certainly required – as provided by the canal and pond – it needed to be balanced by more informally treated vistas on either side.

Using workers from the estate and the family's vineyards, and working during the calmer winter months, the task of opening up these three vistas is still being carried out. In time the canal with its rectangular pool will also be restored. These bodies of water are fed by the River Drée via

an ingenious lock, the hydraulics of which date from the nineteenth century, and possibly earlier. The water from the river flows towards the château in a constant but imperceptible stream, running down the length of the canal and into the pool before descending back to the river along a subterranean channel.

The existing pool is small and almost impossible to see from the château. When it is restored it will be larger so as to bring it back into scale with the château. When forming part of such grandiose architecture, and when set in such a vast space, such statements in water should be strong and clear or else not made at all.

We also went to work on the western side of the château, where the front gates stand. On turning off the public road one passes between two large buildings containing the stables, garages and accommodation for estate workers before reaching the château. Here the 300-metre drive is flanked by a series of yew topiaries which, with age, had begun to look like two rows of dark-green pudding bowls.

Yew is a wonderful plant because it lives for many hundreds of years and tolerates being cut back to a remarkable degree. We decided to cut these oversized topiaries severely to persuade them to grow into cones. Now several years later, they are beginning to comply.

In front of each building stood a line of ancient pleached lime trees, *Tilia × europaea*. I felt they had outlived their usefulness. Unlike pleached hornbeams, pleached limes tend to become coarse-looking in old age. And these had been indifferently pruned over the years, adding to their misery. Furthermore, they hid the

ABOVE *Because the moat is hidden from view on this west front of the château, it is the only part of the garden in which water does not play a role. We removed untidy pleached lime trees from the front of each of the two buildings called* les communs, *and these will be replaced with pleached hornbeams. In the meantime, .cones are being created out of the yews flanking the drive at the right of the picture.*

façade of each building, which was a great shame. After a year's careful consideration, we finally decided to fell them, with the intention of planting hornbeams in their place. In contrast, a double row of lime trees at the western extremity of each building had not been quite so severely pleached, and had remained attractive trees. Equally ancient, they make a most worthwhile contribution to the entrance to the château, and their existence has never been threatened.

Beyond the entrance gate, and across the public road, there had once been an impressive tree-lined drive, which could be seen on old plans. One of our priorities was to replant this drive as soon as possible, and

I drew up a plan for a double avenue of oak or plane trees to line its length of one kilometre to the château.

As a result of the encouragement and help of Comte Bernard de La Rochefoucauld, president of the Fondation Parcs de France, it was the Regional Contingent from Dijon, in concert with several other government bodies, that funded and undertook the drive's restoration. Unfortunately the bureaucracy decided to plant lime trees, *Tilia × europaea*, and these to date have not responded well in this particular location.

On the south side of the château are the main reception rooms and, in its own tower, the small family chapel. From here, one looks out beyond the moat, onto a rectangular lawn surrounded by large trees, where there is a marble statue of Maréchal MacMahon. Here I have designed a formal parterre which, once it is planted, will have the statue as its focal point. We considered felling the trees behind this statue to create a vista through the garden to the spire of the nearby village church, but since the church dates from the nineteenth century and is not exceptional, we decided to leave the surrounding trees and thus increase the visual importance of the parterre. Here there will be rose beds enclosed by box hedges, and gravel paths. It is planned that the entire scheme will be framed by yew hedges two metres high on three sides.

[157]

At an angle of forty-five degrees from the spire of the village church is a remarkable twelfth-century Romanesque chapel. Until recently it, too, was invisible from the château. However, in January 1997 we started felling some of the garden's self-seeded trees in order to create an informal vista from the family chapel in the château to its counterpart in the garden. Reluctant to commit themselves irretrievably to this course of action without careful consideration, the Magentas stopped the felling just short of actually creating the vista. Wisely, they then waited a year, imagining the effect of the vista in each of the four seasons. Finally they made the decision to cut down the remaining twenty-two saplings.

On the northern side of the château, where the River Drée comes closest, it is possible from the rooms of the house to watch the white Charolais cattle grazing in the meadow just beyond the moat. Below the meadow there is a large and rather sinister marsh, at the centre of which stands a group of wellingtonias. We plan to create an informal lake around these trees, thus placing them on an island. Behind the proposed lake an arched stone bridge of considerable beauty leads from Sully to the village of Arnay-le-Duc. I would like to create an informal vista from the château to this bridge. It would balance our recently created vista to the Romanesque chapel on the southern side.

The fundamental question in designing the garden of a historic château like Sully is how far one should go in respecting the designs of previous centuries. There are a number of important issues to be considered.

Firstly, the garden at Sully has changed with each succeeding generation of owners for hundreds of years. With periodical changes in taste – and the inevitability of growth and decay – the garden has always been in a state of flux. Therefore, which of the many periods does one settle upon in making a final decision to re-create the past?

Secondly, although open to the public, Sully is a private house. Many of the garden's former designs are so grandiose, with such elaborate parterres of *plates-bandes aux arabesques* and *broderies*, that it would require a team of at least ten gardeners, aided by every possible machine, to maintain the park along these lines today.

And, finally, why should we be obliged to restore gardens precisely to past designs? In the formal French style of gardening as exercised by Le Nôtre, château and garden blend together, forming a single entity under a strictly codified set of rules and precedents. Accordingly, the château commands the surrounding landscape, representing the authority of its owner. The fact that the entire garden is visible from the house further reinforces the subordinate position of the landscape. Unwanted natural features are subjugated, and most of the plants are clipped and trained. Le Nôtre's two great masterpieces, Vaux-le-Vicomte and

OPPOSITE *As a result of recent and extensive tree-felling, the Romanesque chapel in the garden can now be seen from the south front of the château.* ABOVE *A kilometre-long avenue of lime trees was designed on the west front of the château as an allée d'honneur leading up to the front door.*

Versailles, still reflect this rather uncompromising philosophy. Today, we can admire these two gardens as the magnificent monuments they are, but find they have little of real consequence to say in our own times. Whilst the best-designed gardens respect the houses they frame and take into account the surrounding natural environment, they are also of the age in which they were planted and thereby belong.

At Sully, a garden for the new millennium should neither ignore the past nor treat it lightly: it should be imaginatively designed with an eye to the future. Whereas in the late nineteenth century vast areas of lawn were mown at Sully, today with the use of ha-has and simple wrought-iron fences, livestock from the farm can be brought into the garden and almost up to the château itself. The sight of the white Charolais cattle brings the garden to life in an enchanting way. The added advantage is that many hectares of otherwise unutilised pasture are added to the farm, and the huge expense of mowing the grass is avoided.

The scale of the garden at Sully is so large that one must never forget to make clear, strong and simple statements. Unless they are clear, any additions to the garden will be lost in the immensity of space and be rendered meaningless. And unless they are simple and strong they risk looking trite, which is surely the worst fate of all.

The philosophy behind my designs for the garden at Sully is the same as that for other gardens I have designed, with the exception that here – as a result of the château's symmetry, and also the long history of formality in the garden – formality takes precedence over informality. But this formality is being imposed in a rather relaxed fashion, with greater use being made of indigenous trees than has been the case in the gardens of French châteaux for centuries. Gardens that are too severely formal – like many of those of seventeenth-century France – are imposed upon the landscape, and often lack respect for the underlying genius of the place. By contrast, the magic of the garden at Courances, itself a seventeenth-century landscape, lies in the fact that its formality is imposed sufficiently lightly as to enhance, rather than destroy, the garden's strong sense of place. And just as for the last half-century the garden at Courances has been made less formal and more practical to maintain in a number of subtle ways, so I see Sully being developed in an even more relaxed fashion.

OPPOSITE *Beneath a grove of plane trees – recently liberated from a thick copse of self-seeded saplings – the grazing Charolais cattle create just the sort of pastoral scene that is the spirit of the garden being designed at Sully.*

ACKNOWLEDGEMENTS

Firstly I wish to thank Mr Walter Montagu-Douglas-Scott, who read the manuscript on numerous occasions, and who – in bringing to bear his wisdom and unique perspective of Australia, England and Scotland – made countless improvements. Mr Hugh Main, a fellow landscape designer, also read the manuscript and gave extremely sound advice.

My sincere thanks to my publisher, Ms Julie Gibbs, for having the courage to take on this project; and my editors, Ms Laurie Critchley and Ms Helen Pace, for their patience and sense of humour. Thanks also to my book designer, Ms Ellie Exarchos, for her instinctive and unfailing eye; and to my agent, Mrs Jill Hickson, and her assistants, Sophie and Gaby.

For his excellent photographs of the Woodland and Vegetable gardens (which set such a high standard for me to attempt in vain to emulate), I must thank Mr Balthazar Korab. Likewise I wish to thank Mr Scott Cameron, Mr Jerry Harpur, Mrs Joanne Morris, Mr Craig Kinder, Señor Ignacio Naon and Mr Andrés Sánchez for their superb photographs of my gardens.

I thank the Duc and Duchesse de Magenta; Comte Charles de Ganay; Sir Francis Dashwood, Bart.; Mr Michael Ball; Mr and Mrs James Erskine; Mr Ray Keppie; Mr and Mrs Kerry Packer; Mr and Mrs Gunther Rembel; Mr and Mrs Chris Swain; Mrs Linda Taubman; and Mr and Mrs David Wordsworth for their great assistance.

Nor must I forget the contributions made by the Marquise de Ganay; the Earl of Snowdon; Francesca (Dudu), Baroness von Thielmann; Commander Philip Stonor; Captain Martin Horsford; Mr William Fraser; Mr David Glenn; Monsieur Bertrand Gruss; Madame Andrée Putman and Mr Bill Seal. Again, my sincere thanks to Mr Nick Gall for the excellence of his legal advice, and for sending me his gardening boots – in which I seriously doubt he has ever gardened! – from Hong Kong to London.

I also thank Mrs Rosie Atkins, for her sound opinions on the chapters of the manuscript that she read; Mrs Felicity Green, for her strong and invaluable words on captions; Mr Charles Hulse for the compelling – if unprintable – adjectives he used to describe the effect that too many Latin plant names might have on the text; and the Venerable Rakkhita of the Island Hermitage in Sri Lanka, for showing me the world from a Buddhist perspective.

Finally, I would like to recognise the contribution made by my brother, Kerry, in helping to prompt childhood memories; by the late Laurence Le Guay in taking some of the black-and-white photographs at Greenmount, Candelo; and by the late Mrs Jacqueline Kennedy Onassis, who was the first to suggest the idea of a semi-autobiographical review of my career as a gardener.

INDEX

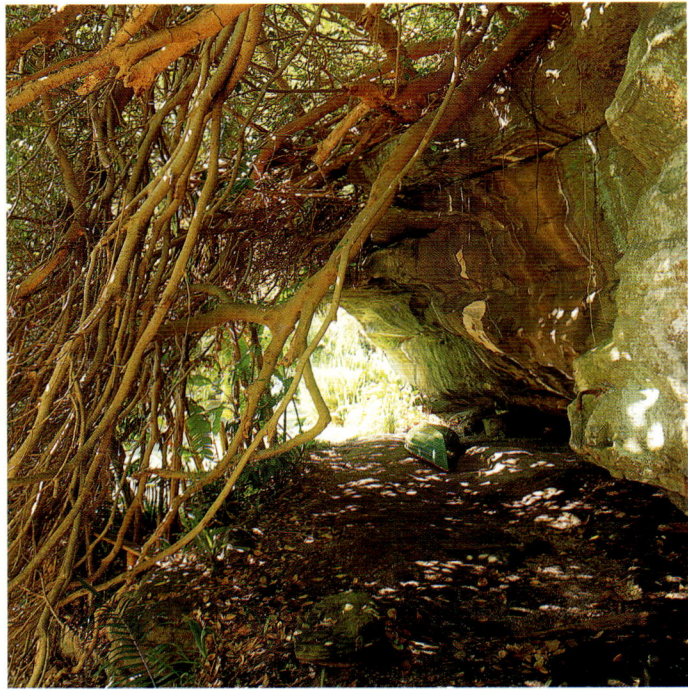